# THE
# TEMPERAMENT
# GOD
# GAVE YOUR
# KIDS

THE
TEMPERAMENT
GOD
GAVE YOUR
KIDS

# THE
# TEMPERAMENT
# GOD
# GAVE YOUR
# KIDS

## Motivate, Discipline, and Love Your Children

### *Art & Laraine Bennett*

OUR SUNDAY VISITOR PUBLISHING DIVISION
OUR SUNDAY VISITOR, INC.
HUNTINGTON, INDIANA 46750

ISBN: 978-1-61278-545-5 (Inventory No. T1244)
eISBN: 978-1-61278-207-2
LCCN: 2011941980

Cover design: Lindsey Riesen
Cover image: Veer
Interior design: Dianne Nelson

PRINTED IN THE UNITED STATES OF AMERICA

*For Lianna, Ray and Laura, Sam, and Lucy*
*and*
*in memory of William Etchemendy*
*(1920-2011)*

# Contents

# Contents

# ACKNOWLEDGMENTS

We are deeply grateful to our children — Lianna, Ray (and his wife, Laura), Sam, and Lucy — for giving us the opportunity to be parents, for being a source of endless inspiration, and for being such good sports. Their wonderful personalities and lively spirits make our lives so rich!

We want to thank our editor at Our Sunday Visitor, Cindy Cavnar, who has stayed in touch with us over the years and with whom we finally are able to publish a book. She is a joy to work with!

We also wish to thank all our friends who shared their own temperament stories with us, especially Robin Sobrak-Seaton and Beth Moschetto.

# INTRODUCTION

*If a man is fully cognizant of his temperament,*
*he can learn easily to direct and control himself.*
*If he is able to discern the temperament of others,*
*he can better understand and help them.*
FATHER CONRAD HOCK

D o you have a child who is "into" everything? As a toddler, he climbs out of his highchair, wails when confined to a car seat, and eagerly explores his surroundings — while you chase him. As a schoolchild, he is talkative, curious, friendly with everyone — and distractible! Your energetic, bubbly child is often the center of attention — and sometimes in the middle of trouble!

Or perhaps you have a child who is just the opposite: quiet, studious, and slow to warm up in social situations. This gentle "old soul" is serious and very sensitive. Too much activity can cause him to be overwrought, and it takes him a while to wind down. He prefers reading or quiet, solitary activities, and he is happy with one good friend.

Then there's the future lawyer: that argumentative, willful child who sometimes makes you want to pull your hair out. Little Patton takes charge over his peers and siblings, is never satisfied with "Because I said so, that's why," and is convinced he is always *right*.

Or perhaps (praise God!) yours is that "one in a million": a sweet, cooperative, and obedient child; agreeable and easygoing at all times. He is undemanding and beloved by his siblings and friends. He sits quietly in the corner, carefully arranging his Matchbox cars, as his siblings and friends create chaos around him.

If yours is a large Catholic family, it is even more likely that you have been blessed with one (or more) of each of the above, as our family has been. You may have been perplexed by the discovery that the same two parents have produced such uniquely individual progeny. You may have these thoughts: "Where did this child come from?" "Why isn't he just like me?" "Am I doing something wrong?"

You are not doing anything wrong, and there is very likely nothing wrong with your child. The differences described above are all differences in God-given temperament. When you understand your child's unique temperament, you will have the key to unlocking his or her behavior, moods, and motivational forces.

In our first book, *The Temperament God Gave You*, we reintroduced the concept of the classic four temperaments: choleric, melancholic, sanguine, and phlegmatic. We showed how understanding our own temperament helps us grow in self-knowledge, improve our relationships with our friends and family, motivate our children, and deepen our spiritual life. In our second book, *The Temperament God Gave Your Spouse*, we looked at all the different combinations of temperaments between spouses and explored how temperament interactions affect spousal communication.

In this book we will take a look at how the four temperaments manifest themselves in children; how your parental temperament meshes with that of your child; how temperament impacts your child's socialization and discipline; how best to motivate your child — in school, at home, and in his social life — by understanding his temperament; and how you can encourage your children to grow in virtue.

## What Is Temperament?

Our temperament is part of our God-given nature, our predisposition to react in certain ways — our default setting, so to speak. How quickly do we react to a person or an idea? How strongly do we react when we are praised or chastised or when we are pressed for an opinion? Are we easygoing or easily angered? Do we tend to look on the bright side, or do we take a more pessimistic approach? Are we readily distracted or intensely focused? Do we thrive on social situations, or would we rather spend a quiet evening at home with a good book? Differences in mood, sociability, emotionality, and persistence are different aspects of our God-given temperament.

Given the same circumstances or stimuli, different children will react differently because of their temperament. Temperamental biases can be observed in infants as young as four months of age[1] and have been found to impact a youngster's sociability, attention to schoolwork, adaptation to new situations, reaction to stress, and other behaviors.

## Blame It on the Greeks!

The concept of temperament dates back more than two thousand years to Hippocrates, the "father" of medical science. Hippocrates believed that differences in personality were physically based, and he identified four temperaments based on the predominant bodily fluid, or humor. Although this was a primitive system of classification, and we no longer recognize the concept of bodily humors, his insights marked the beginning of millennia of research and theory about human personality. And so, from the start, the sanguine temperament was thought to be eager and optimistic; the melancholic, reticent and somewhat doleful; the choleric, passionate; and the phlegmatic, calm.

Cholerics and sanguines have quick reactions, while phlegmatics react slowly, less intensely. Melancholics and cholerics have intense responses, though melancholics are unique because their overt responses tend to be delayed while growing in intensity internally. Phlegmatics and melancholics are introverted — that is, they feel more comfortable with their inner world of thoughts and feelings than with external expressions. Cholerics and sanguines are extraverted — that is, they are energized by, and interact more with, the external, social world.

Though we no longer think of personality the way Hippocrates did, the concept of temperament as a set of biologically based inborn traits or tendencies that underlie our responses to life experiences is still studied today. One noted contemporary psychologist, Dr. Jerome Kagan of Harvard University, had for many years advocated the primacy of environment in personality development, but he became convinced by the research that showed temperament in fact played a key role.[2]

Psychologists continue to debate exactly how biology (the genetic traits we're born with, including temperament) and our environment (education, culture, family of origin, and so on) impact the development of our personality. Regardless of the precise manner in which this happens, we can safely say that the human personality is a dynamic interaction between biological and environmental factors, among which temperament ranks significantly. Most important for us as Catholic parents, it is vital to remember that the human person is never *determined* by his environment or his biology but is fundamentally free. That is, our God-given temperament significantly influences our emotions and behavior, as does our environment, yet we are created by God to be masters of our own actions. As the *Catechism of the Catholic Church* states, "By free will one shapes one's own life" (CCC 1731).

## Contemporary Thoughts on Temperament

In the mid-twentieth century, psychologists and psychiatrists were still operating under the Freudian principle that parents caused their children's behavior, especially maladaptive behaviors. Many believed that the infant was a *tabula rasa*, a blank form that was ultimately shaped — or misshaped! — by his parents or the environment. Psychiatrists Stella Chess and Alexander Thomas, pioneers in the study of temperament in the 1950s, brought everyone back to the commonsense understanding that each child is born with distinct temperamental characteristics. These influence the way he reacts to his surroundings — even as a small child. One child sleeps peacefully through the night while another is fretful and cranky and needs help falling asleep. One toddler easily handles new situations and people, while another anxiously hides behind Mom.

Chess and Thomas discovered that temperamental differences were apparent as early as six months of age. They found that some babies were so *persistent* that they could not be distracted from an object of interest (we would call them melancholic), but other babies could easily be diverted by a new toy (sanguine). Besides distractibility and persistence, Chess and

Thomas identified other characteristics related to temperament: activity, intensity, mood, adaptability, and sociability.[3] Through their pioneering research, Chess and Thomas validated the concept of an inborn temperament, reaffirmed the important relationship between the individual and her environment, and helped parents and educators understand how to work with children and adults of different, sometimes difficult, temperaments.

## Babies Come With Unique Personalities

As a parent realizes that his child is reacting within a normal range of his temperament, the parent is reassured; he no longer thinks, "There is something wrong with my child" or "I must be a terrible parent." When he realizes that the child is exhibiting temperamental issues particular to that temperament, the parent is better able to find workable solutions, to learn how to *work with* that child's particular temperament and, instead of exacerbating the problem, achieve the best results.

For example, when our first child, Lianna, was a baby, she often had difficulty going to sleep, especially if she had been around many people or enjoyed a lot of new activities. She always seemed perfectly happy while meeting new people or taking part in activities, but later she would be wound up and fretful. We learned to adjust our socializing and schedule so that she would not become overwrought and we would not have to be up half the night, walking the halls. There was nothing "wrong" with her; it was part of her constitution. As we later discovered when we learned about temperaments, she is a melancholic, and her behavior was typical for that temperament.

Recent studies[4] have shown that children with anxious temperaments may be more likely to experience problems with depression and anxiety later on in life. Early intervention, however, can prevent this — for example, teaching an anxious child how to calm himself, to replace negative thinking patterns with positive ones, to separate realistic from unrealistic thoughts, and to learn new ways of handling strong negative emotions. Recognizing potential temperamental weaknesses early on can be greatly beneficial to the child's healthy development.

## The Gift of Temperament

Each child comes into this world already equipped with a special gift from God: his temperament. God knows just what temperament your child needs to fulfill his mission on earth, and just what temperament will help you, his parent, grow in holiness. You can help your children make the most of this gift, discover their talents, grow in virtue, and become their best, true self. With your love and God's grace, they will.

In addition, by understanding your child's temperament and your own, seeing how your temperaments click or clash, and adjusting accordingly, you will have a heads-up in terms of making the parenting process a smooth road instead of an ongoing battle. A recent study by University of Washington psychologists discovered that children whose parents adjusted their parenting style to suit their child's temperament had happier and better-adjusted children.[5] Children whose parents had an inflexible parenting style — particularly when that style was harsh and critical — were more likely to suffer from anxiety and depression, particularly if the child had low levels of fear (we would call them choleric) or was particularly prone to frustration and irritability (melancholic). On the other hand, children who had difficulty with self-control (sanguine) needed firm parental guidance. In Chapter 6, we will help you discover what your parental temperament is, and in Chapter 7, we will discuss in greater detail the interaction between parent and child, depending on their different temperaments. In Chapter 8, we will bring it all together to show how we parents can encourage virtue in our children.

In the long run, understanding your child's temperament and learning to work *with* him, as opposed to fighting him, will help you challenge, motivate, and teach your child most effectively. Sometimes you will have to go outside your own "temperament box" in order to be the coach, teacher, protector, or advocate that your child needs. Eventually, God willing, your child will grow in grace and virtue, developing his natural virtues and learning some new ones to navigate the sea of life.

***

In the next chapter, we will take a closer look at the classic four temperaments, particularly in the way they tend to be manifested in children. Most people are a combination of temperaments, typically a primary and secondary temperament.[6] Yet every individual is unique, free to cooperate with God's grace and to decide whether to respond according to his temperament or otherwise. The idealized "types" presented here are meant simply as guidelines to help you discover your own temperament, which is only one aspect of your total personality, and that of your child. The four types are a tool, a shortcut to understanding your child's primary motivations, needs, and tendencies. The objective is never to put people or children in a box — actually, to do so would be detrimental to a young child's developing self-concept.

In fact, by understanding temperament and how it influences our behavior and reactions, we are *less* likely to find ourselves stuck in a box. We will identify our strengths and weaknesses as well as ways to motivate ourselves and our kids to grow in virtue, moving beyond the knee-jerk reactions triggered by our temperamental tendencies. But first, we need to figure out our children's temperaments.

■ ■ ■

*Why should you understand your children's temperaments? Because that knowledge will help you:*

- *Understand rather than blame yourself or your child for what is a temperament-related issue: some kids are more active than others, some are more emotional, other have difficulty adapting to new situations.*
- *Identify behavior that is "normal" for each temperament.*
- *Anticipate potentially difficult or stressful situations for each temperament.*
- *Identify weaknesses of each temperament and ways to strengthen those areas.*
- *Learn how to motivate and discipline different temperaments.*
- *Identify potential areas of conflict between your temperament and your child's temperament.*
- *Appreciate the fact that temperaments are a gift from God.*

■ ■ ■

# CHAPTER 1

# TEMPERAMENT AND
# YOUR CHILD

*To know the temperaments of our fellow men helps us to
understand them better, treat them more correctly,
bear with them more patiently.*

FATHER CONRAD HOCK

Angela and Dan came in for counseling with their teenage son, Zach.[1] They were concerned about Zach's performance in school: he was easily distracted, was constantly
texting his friends and making after-school plans without con-
sulting his parents, and his room was a complete disaster. "I
think we should have him tested for ADHD," said Angela.

Angela and Dan were themselves quiet and rather schol-
arly. Angela kept a meticulous home, and Dan was an engineer. They much preferred spending quiet evenings reading
rather than going to parties or socializing. They tolerated their
son's participation in sports and his many school activities, but
they wondered whether his distractedness, disorderliness, and
his difficulty persevering through long, tedious school projects were symptoms of a serious problem. "He is so different
from us!" exclaimed Angela.

All parents at one time or another (perhaps even on a
daily basis!) find themselves in the puzzling position that
Angela and Dan were in. Sometimes we scratch our heads,

saying: "Where did this kid come from? I was never like that as a child!" Perhaps we find ourselves butting heads or locked in conflict over what should have been a simple request. We may wonder why the air in our home seems so tense around one particular child or why another child seems so unmotivated.

The key to solving these often perplexing interactions is to recognize that each of our children is born with his own unique temperament. Our kids are not Mini-Me's. When we realize that many of his puzzling reactions may in fact be considered normal for that child's temperament, we can relax and learn to relate to him according to his unique personality, and we can develop strategies that help him address his temperament's weaknesses.

As a document from the Pontifical Council for the Family states, "Each child is a unique and unrepeatable person and must receive individualized formation."[2] Amy Chua, author of the controversial best-selling book *Battle Hymn of the Tiger Mother*, says her biggest regret was not recognizing her daughters' individual temperaments. She nearly lost her daughters completely through her one-size-fits-all parenting style.[3]

> Sometimes we scratch our heads, saying: "Where did this kid come from?"

As parents, we want our children to be happy; we know that their ultimate happiness is the fruit of doing God's will and, eventually, of finding eternal happiness in heaven. In order to reach that goal, it is essential that they learn to make wise decisions about their lives and use their free will as a force for truth and goodness. If we help them grow in self-knowledge, in self-mastery, and in virtue, we will give them the means to remain faithful to their baptismal vows and capable of fulfilling their vocation to love. As the Pontifical Council for the Family also notes, "education in love ... is at the same time education of one's spirit, one's sensitivity, and one's feelings."[4]

## Each Child Is Unique

Part of the individualized formation that we provide as parents, therefore, includes recognizing each child's unique temperamental needs, emotions, and natural virtues and strengths. We need to understand the whole person: his or her emotions, spirit, and sensitivities. With this understanding, we can motivate, discipline, and teach more effectively according to each temperament, with fewer power struggles, meltdowns, and crises.

If we insist on making a "lefty" throw balls or write with his right hand, we will encounter a lot more frustration, and the child may not reach the potential he would have had he been writing or pitching from his natural strength. The same holds true for temperament.

As it turns out, Zach did not have attention deficit disorder; instead, he turned out to be a rather distractible, sociable, and impulsive sanguine. Angela and Dan were just the opposite — quiet, reflective, meticulous melancholics. They discovered through counseling that a major source of conflict with their teenage son was, quite simply, their very different temperaments and unrealistic expectations. This was a great relief to them. Understanding how Zach's temperament affected his behavior and reactions helped diffuse many arguments and reassured his parents that Zach was neither "bad" nor intentionally provocative. Angela and Dan discovered that tasks that would have come naturally to them (being organized, starting school projects) are, in fact, quite difficult for kids of a sanguine temperament. Their counselor suggested some practical tips and strategies that would help them guide Zach in his efforts to become more organized and mindful.

## Goodness of Fit

Psychiatrists Stella Chess and Alexander Thomas, whose landmark studies put temperament in the spotlight, discovered that the *interaction* between a parent's and a child's temperament sometimes proved pivotal to the quality of the parent-child relationship. They called the match (or mismatch) between parents (or environment) and children "goodness of fit," because it explained many frustrations and even conflicts that families sometime experience due to temperament interactions.[5] For example, a very argumentative and strong-willed child may baffle and frustrate an easygoing parent who concludes that there must be something wrong with this intense child. On the other hand, a very decisive, intense choleric parent might be frustrated with a slow-moving, easygoing child and assume he is lazy or unproductive. An extraverted, sociable sanguine parent, when faced with a quiet, slow-to-warm-up melancholic, may worry that his child is anti-social. And sparks are sure to fly when high-powered, intense, and demanding parents are faced with equally intense, demanding children.

Parents who assume that their kids should respond in exactly the same way as they respond are likely to find themselves exceedingly frustrated. They might be tempted to punish a child for the way the child is hardwired. Certain temperamental characteristics are part of a child's DNA and simply can't be changed. For example, a child who reacts very intensely may cry longer than other children and may resist being soothed. This is not a willful decision nor should it be a punishable offense. A shy child can't help being hesitant around strangers and may struggle to give eye contact. Again, you wouldn't punish him for this, but would, instead, gently encourage him to take steps to overcome his shyness. Just as you wouldn't reprimand a child for being mild and easygoing or slow-paced, you shouldn't admonish a high-energy child for her energy level. As Dr. Jerome Kagan said: "Had the parents of Lyndon Johnson and Bill Clinton tried to mute their sons' extreme extraversion, those men might not have become president."[6]

On the other hand, we shouldn't fall prey to the erroneous belief that what is natural or inborn can't be formed, directed, or channeled. Knowing a child's temperamental strengths and weaknesses gives parents a heads-up on their child's natural gifts and those virtues their child should be encouraged to acquire.

With the information in this book, even natural opposites (according to temperament) can learn to get along and even to appreciate each other's gifts. Zach's parents decided to get him a tutor with whom he would meet during study hall to help him stay on top of all his various long-term projects. Zach learned how to break big projects into smaller, manageable chunks and was encouraged to start these projects earlier. He sat down with his parents to weed out some of the less important activities so that he would have some evenings when he stayed home for family time and to catch up on his chores.

For their part, Zach's parents learned to be more accepting of their son's highly sociable nature and to encourage him to bring his friends over more often. Though they still found it difficult to understand why he needed to spend every waking moment either conversing with friends or doing some activity, they began to appreciate his gift of extraversion and the new life and enthusiasm it brought to their hitherto quiet home.

Let's take a quick look at the classic four temperaments as they are manifested in children. Bear in mind that this is a brief overview and that most people are a blend of temperaments. In subsequent chapters, we will take an in-depth look at each of the four temperaments and the issues surrounding learning styles, emotions, discipline, and motivation for each of the temperaments.

■ ■ ■

### The Four Temperaments in a Nutshell

*You are at church when one of your children fails to genuflect. A sibling[7]*

a. *Punches him (Choleric).*
b. *Tattles to Mom (Melancholic).*
c. *Demonstrates how he would do it, talking all the while (Sanguine).*
d. *Ignores it (Phlegmatic).*

■ ■ ■

## THE CHOLERIC

Your choleric child comes into the world ready to challenge the Org Chart and take charge. He is strong-willed, determined, a quick learner, and a natural leader. Cholerics are dynamic, self-motivated, and confident — even when they may not have the experience that warrants it! They always have an opinion, and they never hesitate to express it. Their reactions are quick, strong, and sustained, making them very persistent when they are pursuing a goal — or arguing with their parents. Our friend Susan says that when her seven-year-old choleric daughter gets together with her equally choleric friend, "It's like Stalin and Lenin on a play date!"

The flip side is that cholerics can be impatient, stubborn, interruptive, quick-tempered, and occasionally lacking in empathy. And they can be *annoyingly* persistent and opinionated. The defining feature of the choleric is that they love to argue.

Try not to take it personally. Young cholerics sharpen their baby teeth on debates, grabbing hold of an opinion like a puppy playing tug-of-war with a sock. Sometimes it's best just to let them tussle. Parents of all temperaments tend to be alarmed when faced with argumentative children; they assume that the child is disrespectful of their authority or, worse, is an incipient anarchist. But with a choleric child this is usually not the case.

When Lucy (a choleric, like her mom) was twelve, she became concerned about the shape of her head. She was studying herself in the mirror with a worried expression.

"Mom, I think my head is shaped weird," she said.

"No, it's not," Laraine replied, without looking. "Your head is supposed to look like that."

"But look at the way it is sort of rounded, behind my ears," she insisted.

"What are you talking about? It is *supposed* to be round behind your ears!" Laraine retorted impatiently. "If your head went straight back behind your ears, you'd look like a Martian!"

"Martians' heads don't go straight *back* behind their ears," argued Lucy, instantly diverted from the topic at hand. "They go straight *up* from their heads, like this." Lucy demonstrated the lightbulb-shaped outline of a classic Martian head.

"Not *those* Martians," Laraine argued in reply. "I'm talking about the *other* Martians — the ones whose heads go straight *back* from their ears!"

"What are you two arguing about?" interrupted sanguine Sam, who had been listening in bemusement. "Neither of you has ever *seen* a Martian!" Which was true, but by that time the two cholerics were in full-on debate mode.

The choleric child tends to do well in school (provided there is not a learning disability) because he enjoys competition, likes to excel, and is a quick learner. Cholerics also tend to be the ones leading the rest of the class. Though we had homeschooled our older children for a number of years, by the time Lucy was due to enter third grade she had had enough. The circle of influence was too small for her choleric-sanguine personality. We finally sent her to school, and each day as Laraine picked her up she would jump in the car and exclaim, "That was the *best* day of my life!"

If you are becoming frustrated with a strong-willed choleric child, it is sometimes helpful to remind yourself not to get caught up in secondary power struggles; power struggles rarely impart the lesson you are hoping to instill and may instead provoke obstinacy in the choleric. Ultimately, the goal is not to attain what *you* want but to enable your child to do what *God* wants.[8] The strong will that often frustrates you as a parent is the same will that can say no to undesirable peer pressure and has guided many of the saints to heroic virtue. As a parent, you can lead your choleric along the right path by appealing to his *reason* and by giving him *supernatural motivation*. One day, your quick-witted, strong-willed child may become a leader for Christ and the Church.

# The Melancholic

Melancholics are sensitive, artistic, and serious, and they require plenty of space, quiet, and solitude. The melancholic is the most reflective and introverted of all the temperaments. Thus, a melancholic will need plenty of time to think things through or to process what he has learned and experienced during the day. He will need a quiet and private space in order to "regroup" after a busy day at school or playing with other children. This child needs to be gently encouraged to express and extend himself.

Before we understood the temperaments, we ourselves were rather oblivious about the particular needs and sensitivities of this delicate temperament. We lived in Germany for a few years while Art was managing a mental health program for military families overseas. While there, we put our firstborn, a sweet and sensitive melancholic, in German kindergarten. Lianna was only three and a half and was particularly ill equipped, by temperament and language, to defend herself against the rough, pushy kids. Chess and Thomas' research shows that throwing a shy, slow-to-warm-up child into a large, raucous social situation will not help the child overcome his shyness and is more likely to cause him to withdraw further. The best approach is to *gradually* introduce challenging experiences so that the timid child can successfully master new social situations. Since we didn't know any of this, we subjected our daughter to an unduly stressful and upsetting situation, because *we* wanted her to have a cross-cultural experience.

The melancholic child is slow to react, but the reaction will be intense and long lasting when it comes. At first, he may not seem to react at all, but by the time his reaction is perceptible it is already deeply felt and vehemently held. As Father Conrad Hock describes it, a melancholic's reactions are like a post being driven into the earth; with each blow, the post is driven more firmly into the ground of their soul.[9] Because the melancholic child's reactions are slow, a parent may mistakenly assume that the child is not listening or is even willfully disobedient. To punish such a child for his temperamentally slow reaction would be perceived by your melancholic child as the height of injustice. Fairness is critical to the melancholic child; principle, detail, and order are paramount.

The weaknesses of this temperament are that he or she can be moody and withdrawn, overly self-conscious, and perfectionist. Critical of himself and others, the melancholic child can also be fearful of initiating new things. He may seem aloof or overly sensitive to other kids, and they might take advantage of him by playing tricks on him or making him the scapegoat.

The melancholic child needs a gentle touch, patience, and sensitivity in child rearing, and he will be especially responsive to your efforts to walk alongside him in teaching him new skills and initiating new projects. The melancholic child who is given loving support and encouragement will blossom. Like a fine wine, your melancholic child just needs time to mature into an accomplished adult.

# The Sanguine

The sanguine child is eager, bright, sensitive, funny, fun loving, and enthusiastic: in short, the life of the party and the center of attention. He is a quick learner, equally quick to react, and rarely bears a grudge. He is eager to please and wants everyone to be happy. Fun and attention are prime motivators. The sanguine child wears his heart on his sleeve: you will see in his expressive face the swift fluctuation of moods, emotions, ideas, and impulses. All children need love and appreciation, but the sanguine child *overtly* expresses this need, certainly more so than children of other temperaments.[10]

The sanguine is diametrically opposed to the melancholic in every way: where the melancholic is introverted, the sanguine is extraverted; where the melancholic is detailed, careful, and quiet, the sanguine is disorganized, distracted, and boisterous. (Letting these polar opposites share a room, if they are siblings, is a recipe for disaster!)

Sanguine children need good intellectual and spiritual formation so that they do not become superficial: in this media-dominated age, sanguines are particularly susceptible to being distracted by pop culture and the siren call of the Internet. They have bright, inquisitive minds, but they need close supervision and guidance in academics so that they will stay focused and persevere.

Discipline is necessary for everyone's personal growth, but discipline does not come naturally to the carefree sanguine — especially sustained discipline. The virtues of perseverance and self-denial are crucial to the impulsive, fun-loving sanguine. He will need your help in staying motivated over the long haul. Help him to connect the dots between hard work and true joy, between thoughtful reflection and peace, between temperance and self-mastery.

## THE PHLEGMATIC

Count your blessings for a phlegmatic child! He is a joy — so peaceful, quiet, cooperative, and obedient that you will be forever spoiled. He is quiet, dutiful, and cooperative in school, and he never gets into fights with other children. At home he can entertain himself for hours without requiring attention.

The phlegmatic child is slow to react, and his reactions are typically not intense or long lived. He remains calm even under intense pressure; it takes a long time for anger to build in a phlegmatic. A little brother can annoy and provoke his older phlegmatic sister for days until she will finally inform him, "You are so annoying!" and then become quiet and passive again. The phlegmatic may even take the blame for another sibling's wrongdoing just to avoid the conflict and disharmony that otherwise would ensue. He plays well with others and is usually liked by all unless he is so completely phlegmatic that the other children don't notice him.

You have to watch out, however. Your phlegmatic child can be so cooperative that you may realize, after living with him for ten or twelve years, that you really don't have a clue about what he really thinks or feels. What is his favorite show or pastime? What angers him or frustrates him? What does he talk about with his best friend? Does he even *have* a best friend? If you are blessed with many children, you may end up ignoring the phlegmatic child — he simply goes unnoticed amid the bedlam of a large household. And though he rarely calls attention to himself, this doesn't mean he doesn't *need* that attention.

The phlegmatic tends to be so willing to please that he will gravitate toward whatever activities *other* people want to do. He perseveres in his duties out of a strong sense of cooperation and obligation, rarely if ever out of a desire to impress or influence others. Sometimes the phlegmatic will conform or surrender just to ensure peace, even if it is not in his best interest. Phlegmatics must be encouraged to make up their own minds. But it takes time to draw out what exactly is *in* their minds! For this reason, a phlegmatic child should not be rushed into making important decisions.

The flip side to a quiet, undemanding, pleasant nature is that without proper encouragement, phlegmatic children can become sluggish or unmotivated. In new situations they may lack initiative, requiring more time than other temperaments to become acclimated. Fear of offending, of making the wrong decision, or of creating unnecessary waves can result in serious procrastination — even about important life decisions.

Parents of phlegmatic children need to help them recognize their own talents and gifts, and to use them for the benefit of all. You can encourage your phlegmatic child to take on leadership roles as he gets older. Though he may not seem like a self-starter, once you remind him of his talents (cf. Matthew 25:14-30), he may become emboldened to try. With his thoughtful, reliable, and even-tempered personality, your phlegmatic can become — if he overcomes his natural distaste for conflict and taking charge — an excellent leader. He will tend to lead by example, by serving, and by promoting cooperation from within the ranks. Encouraging a phlegmatic to acquire the virtues of holy boldness, courage, and magnanimity will enable him to become a future leader for Christ.

***

Management theorist Peter Drucker (considered the "father" of modern management) wrote that "a person can perform only from strength. One cannot build performance on weaknesses, let alone on something one cannot do at all."[11] Without minimizing the importance of God's grace in helping each of us overcome our weaknesses, there is a great deal of practical wisdom in this point. Parents will find it far easier to help their children grow emotionally, intellectually, and spiritually when they build on their children's *natural strengths*. As St. Thomas Aquinas put it, grace builds on nature.

Parents can appreciate the choleric's natural leadership and independence, the melancholic's depth and nobility of purpose, the sanguine's generosity and gregariousness, and the phlegmatic's cooperation and peacefulness. Understanding temperament helps parents work with their children's natural strengths, which can then be used as a springboard to develop virtue and to overcome weaknesses.

# CHAPTER 2

# Your Conquering Choleric Child

*It was going to be one of Rabbit's busy days. As soon as he woke up he felt important, as if everything depended upon him. It was just the day for Organizing Something ... a Captainish sort of day, when everybody said, "Yes, Rabbit" and "No, Rabbit," and waited until he had told them.*
A. A. MILNE, *WINNIE-THE-POOH*

B race yourself. You are in for the ride of your life. Your choleric child is a bundle of energy: bright, self-reliant, and demanding, she is often found in the middle of things, taking charge. She is goal-oriented, confident, and strong-willed. She is your future lawyer, CEO, president of the United States.

She is also opinionated, argumentative, stubborn, and bossy.

"Are you listening to me? Did you *hear* what I said?"

"Yes, Lucy, I heard," Mom replies.

"Then why didn't you answer me?" Lucy demands.

## Characteristics of the Choleric Child

According to the ancient Greek classification of everything according to four elements — earth, water, fire, and air

— cholerics were fire. And it's true: their spirits are fiery; their passions, enthusiasms, interests, *and tempers* are quickly ignited. Their reactions are swift, strong, and sure. As a result, cholerics are naturally decisive. Father Conrad Hock wrote, "The choleric is made to rule. He feels happy when he is in a position to command, to draw others to him, and to organize large groups."[1]

**Born to Lead:** Cholerics assume they are in charge at all times. Even when they have no experience. And even when nobody is asking them to take charge. When choleric Mother Angelica decided she was going to build an international television network, she didn't stop to think about whether she had the necessary background, experience, or capital. She plunged right in. To raise money for her order's new foundation in Alabama, Mother Angelica and her nuns sold handmade fishing lures. St. Peter's Fishing Lures were so successful that they were even featured in *Sports Illustrated* — yet she had never fished a day in her life![2] In 1981, when Ronald Reagan was shot, choleric Secretary of State Alexander Haig declared himself in charge. "I am in control here," Haig famously stated, despite not being next in the order of presidential succession.

The same is true for choleric children, budding field marshals and secretaries of state. When they are little, they say things like, "You're not the boss of me!" That's because they think *they* are the bosses of the world. What does experience matter when you have the attitude of a Nikita Khrushchev? My friend Susan laughs when she tells me about seven-year-old choleric Grace. "Yes, Grace, I *do* need to dial 'one' before I call that number.... Yes, I do. I think I would know! ... You're *seven*, Grace!"

One choleric college student met her future spouse when she tutored *him* in Spanish. She was blonde, blue-eyed, and from Southern California, and he was a native Spanish speaker from Mexico. Another choleric recalls that, as an eleven-year-old, she would regularly ground her *older* sister for using her clothes without asking or for failing to clean up messes in the room they shared.

**Goal-Oriented:** Cholerics are fearless and driven when pursuing a goal. Once they have locked in, they are like a heat-seeking missile. Everything not goal-related is ignored. This may be how the choleric gets his reputation for rolling over people or lacking empathy. They simply are so focused on their goal that everything else pales in comparison and falls by the wayside. The choleric plunges relentlessly forward; he rarely whines or complains when faced with obstacles or difficulties, and even views doing so as a weakness.

And throughout, he maintains a positive, can-do attitude.

**Bossy:** Laraine used our daughter Lucy — then a high school sophomore — as an example, when she gave a talk on temperament to the seventh-grade girls at Lucy's school, describing the different temperaments in simple ways they could understand. To explain "bossiness" as a characteristic of cholerics, for example, Laraine said:

Now this doesn't mean you just boss your younger siblings around. It means you like to boss everyone — your teachers, your parents. And when you argue, you argue with everyone — teachers, parents, and friends. Not just your younger siblings.

The seventh-graders were agog at the sheer magnificence of Lucy's choleric ways. Later, Laraine told Lucy about her talk.

"Aw, those poor little seventh-graders! They'll be terrified when they see me in the hall!" She paused and grinned, "*I like it!*"

Some choleric children, however, have difficulty making friends since they tend to be too bossy. Or they make friends with a docile child who obeys their every command and functions as their own personal sidekick, a meek and mousy Robin for the choleric Batman. In a sense, they sometimes seem so independent and self-contained that friendships almost don't seem necessary. Yet friends are important for all children, no matter what their temperament, and wise parents will help their choleric children tone down the bossiness and learn to take turns and share, to listen empathically to their quieter friends, and to recognize their need for others.

**Always Right:** The default setting for cholerics is that they are right. Choleric Rush Limbaugh proudly announces on his radio show that he is proven right, 98 percent of the time. When Lucy was taking our temperament test, she noticed "always right" under the weaknesses section. "But, Dad," she objected, "that's not a weakness!" For confident cholerics, even the weaknesses are perceived as strengths!

**To the Point:** Cholerics are impatient and have a tendency to interrupt other people. This is partly because they assume that they already know where the other person is heading and, in the interest of efficiency, want to cut to the chase. They waste no time beating around the bush. Even young cholerics are efficient in speech and rarely snivel or whine, preferring to state their demands succinctly. They can be blunt. Blogger Simcha Fisher[3] relates a story of her choleric toddler during a meltdown. "I *want* to close the door!" she yelled. Mom calmly responds, "Maybe if you ask me politely, I will move over so you can close it." The three-year-old, sniffling through her tears of rage, asks in her most polite voice, "Mama, will you please move your fat bottom?"

**Impatient:** Cholerics become impatient when other children are too slow, too wishy-washy, too awkward, or too detailed. Lucy of the comic strip *Peanuts* exhibits this classic choleric quality. She cavalierly dispenses "tough love" advice at her psychiatric booth and calls phlegmatic Charlie Brown a "blockhead." In one episode, she demands of Linus, "Why do you do such stupid things?"

"Why do I do stupid things?" Linus ponders thoughtfully. "Why don't I think? What's the matter with me? Where's my sense of responsibility? Then I ask myself, am I really responsible? Is it really my fault when I do something wrong? Must I answer for my mistakes?" Annoyed with the lengthy soul searching, Lucy hauls off and hits him. As he lies on the ground, head spinning, Linus reflects: "Her kind never worries about these things!"[4]

**Practical and Drama-Free:** The choleric capacity for zeroing in on a target also keeps them from drowning in trivia or fruitlessly worrying. Cholerics are resilient, practical, and show a great deal of common sense. At an age when most girls are engaging in overwrought gossip, tears, and melodrama, our daughter Lucy always stayed above the fray. She shrugged off school drama like water flowing off a duck's back. This was not because she is calm and easygoing like a phlegmatic; rather, it's because she doesn't see the *point* in wasting time on silly gossip or girlish dramatics.

She also has a hefty dose of common sense and practical intuition. Once, when she was a preteen, an adult inappropriately asked her to attend a tutoring session — alone. She told Laraine that she felt it wasn't right and just told the teacher she couldn't. Children of other temperaments might not have the self-assurance and mental firmness to stand up for themselves like this.

When our older two children left their lunches at home, Laraine would usually bring the lunches to them at school lest they starve. Not so, the second two. Sam (sanguine) would charm his way into a free lunch, while Lucy would simply request money. "You have to ask the boys," she said philosophically. "Girls are really picky and want you to pay them back."

**Just Do It:** The choleric child will dash off an essay, practice the piano, or wash dishes quickly and vigorously — but not necessarily up to the standards you have set. We finally caught on to Lucy's method of cleaning after finding piles of clothing, books, and old lunch bags under the bed and in the closet. Cholerics take pride in purposeful activity and completing a task — not in perfecting each detail along the way. They would rather jump right in and start assembling the new shelf, painting the wall, or writing the book report, rather than reading the directions, putting down a drop cloth, or finishing the book.

Although cholerics pride themselves on their facility at learning new skills and accomplishing their tasks quickly, if the task proves too daunting or too difficult they can become very angry. Batting practice, penmanship, dance class, art projects, and math lessons may become occasions of great frustration for the impatient choleric who wants to do everything — not perfectly, but immediately and proficiently. These occasions may devolve into tantrums and tears of rage. Or the choleric will say, "This is stupid. Forget it." Cholerics will not blame themselves for these failures, as would the melancholic or phlegmatic child. They blame others (or the stupid task), and then they move on.

## Becoming a Person

Around the age of two, all children embark upon the process of individuation. Toddlers are struggling to assert themselves, to separate themselves from their parents and begin the process of becoming an individual.

Babies don't even realize they are separate from their mothers.[5] Then, at about the age of eighteen months, a child begins to become aware of *himself* as a unique person. This is normal; everyone is familiar with the toddler's favorite word — "No!" Saying no is one way the child tries to differentiate himself from others. A vital part of being a person, created in the image and likeness of God, is the fact that one is free: free to choose for oneself, to be responsible for one's own actions. The small child is not, of course, consciously aware of this, but being able to say no is a developmental step toward becoming responsible, asserting the capacity to choose freely for oneself.

> Wise parents will help their choleric child tone down the bossiness and learn to take turns and share, to listen empathically to their quieter friends, and to recognize their need for others.

This process, however, can be particularly challenging with a choleric child; the choleric child's reactions tend to be stronger, more insistent, and more demanding than those of other temperaments. It's important for parents not to become overly upset by this normal part of development but instead to respond to it with good humor and helpful instruction.[6] It helps to remember that all kids will one day be teens, and all teens will one day be invited to drink at a party, smoke marijuana, or break curfew. We want our kids to be able to say no with confidence.

## LEARNING STYLE, SCHOOL, AND THE CHOLERIC CHILD

Because young cholerics are bold, inquisitive, and eager to learn, they love to ask questions and will challenge answers that don't seem logical to them. This is the way they find out about the world and process information. Some children learn by cautiously observing, hanging back until they have assessed the situation; others learn by asking questions and poking their fingers into things. This is related more to temperament than to gender. One mom we know took her three preschool-age children to an interactive marine lab with fish tanks and touch pools. The oldest, a boy, hung back when it came time to touch the fish in the touch pool, while his younger choleric sister had no qualms about plunging her fingers in to touch the swellshark!

Of course, all children seek reasonable explanations for demands and requirements that teachers and parents place on them, but the choleric especially so. Laraine's mother relates that when Laraine was about three years old, she constantly demanded "Why?" Finally, she asked her mom, "Why do I ask 'Why?' so much?"

When they are older, choleric children may raise their hand and dare to disagree with the teacher. Some teachers appreciate this highly interactive style, while others, of a more authoritarian style, prefer students to sit quietly and take notes. Cholerics are usually quick studies, so they may intuit exactly what is required by each of their teachers. What's the bottom line? They are quick learners with a practical focus.

## A Measure of Control

The older choleric will also enjoy a learning environment that offers an understanding of the big picture, its vision and grand purpose. He's not satisfied filling out tedious forms or doing silly tasks, and he respects a teacher who presents challenging and complex subjects in a fast-paced style without dumbing down the material. And he'll enjoy stimulating class discussions and want to take on the more difficult projects.

The best sort of situation for cholerics is one in which they feel they have at least some control over their learning material and environment. If you are homeschooling, you can involve them in planning their school year, their choice of subjects, or their daily schedule, depending on their age. They are competitive and independent learners who are usually quite capable of taking charge of a project and following it through to the end. A program that allows the student to progress at her own rate affords her the opportunity to speed ahead, quickly mastering the introductory topics so as to delve into the more challenging modules. Other temperaments might lose motivation with nonstructured, independent learning, but not the self-motivated, competitive choleric.

Choleric children have great powers of concentration and are capable of zeroing in on a task and blocking out all else. They enjoy checking things off their list. They might, however, begin looking around for bigger fish to fry than beating their brothers and sisters at math Olympiads or spelling. Ours was bent on going to school as soon as her older brothers and sisters were headed off. She showed the same remarkable persistence about this as she did when she wanted a dog. (For the record, we now own a dog.)

One homeschooling family with several intellectually precocious, choleric children sent their kids to community college as soon as they were sixteen, the minimum required age. Their kids thrived in the college atmosphere, taking classes with adults and kids older than they were and satisfying college requirements before they had even graduated from high school. Homeschooled cholerics (and boys of all temperaments) like the competition that school outside the home offers, especially when they feel they are not being sufficiently challenged.

Finally, participating in sports is important for all children, but especially for choleric children. Let them fight to win on the soccer or lacrosse field, or expend energy in the swimming pool so they are not as often fighting with you. Further, they will learn the importance of doing what Coach says and working as a team — learning obedience and humility, which are important virtues for the independent choleric.

## DISCIPLINING THE CHOLERIC CHILD

Wise parents (or, perhaps, *tired* parents) will try to avoid and diffuse *unnecessary* power struggles with their children. For example, when the toddler says no and refuses to get dressed, you can divert his attention by offering several choices: "Would you like to wear this coat or that one?" "Shall we go first to the grocery store or to the bank?" "Look — fresh vegetables! Why don't you pick out which ones we shall have for dinner to-night?" Cholerics can be challenged: "Let's see if you can pick up ten toys before the timer goes off" or "Let's have a race and see who can get into their pajamas first!"

Often, those children who have the best language skills are the least likely to throw tantrums and otherwise make themselves obnoxious. They are capable of telling their parents why they are frustrated, instead of bawling hysterically. In fact, parents can always encourage the use of words, even with a frustrated, crying, flailing toddler: "Use your words, speak nicely." This way you aren't rewarding bad behavior or whining by acknowledging or giving in to their demands but instead are rewarding calm and respectful requests. Giving toddlers choices and expecting calm use of words often help with youngsters — but when the choleric child is older, reason comes into play.

While we want to help all our children (including the cholerics) to be appropriately expressive of and honest in their opinions, we also want them to be *respectful* in how they disclose them: "I have no problem letting you finish that TV show, but I want you to ask me politely and apologize for yelling" or "I know you want to decide which game you and your friend will play next, but you need to ask nicely and to allow her to have a turn choosing as well" or "How do you think your friend felt when you wouldn't let her play the game she wanted?"

Parents of cholerics can help model patience and perseverance when things are not going their way, and humility. When cholerics encounter a particularly difficult task or need to learn a new skill, they have to learn how to be patient with themselves. Humiliation is anathema to choleric children, yet they must eventually learn humility and patience. Choleric schoolchildren need to learn that the rough draft cannot, in the interest of efficiency, become the final draft. They will not be playing the *Moonlight Sonata* on the second lesson. Impatience and brusqueness in dealing with younger siblings and parents should give way to empathy and respect. Furthermore, cholerics feel a deep need for verbal appreciation and acknowledgment of their achievements.

■ ■ ■

*Instead of "Don't you take that tone with me!" try this: "I'm not going to listen to your request unless you speak to me in a respectful tone of voice."*

■ ■ ■

## The Voice of Reason

We have seen that the choleric is strong-willed and demanding, wanting to have reasons for every directive and willing to engage in arguments when he disagrees. Yet even the most headstrong choleric can heed the voice of reason, to his parent's advantage. Instead of falling back on "Because I said so!" try to engage your choleric through reasonable arguments and compelling goals.

For example, it's bedtime and your choleric is still awake. Remind him that in order to perform well on the test tomorrow, he will need his sleep — and grades are important for getting into the high school or college of his choice. When he balks at vegetables, explain the importance of good nutrition. When he is particularly obstinate, appeal to one of his favorite saints or the Blessed Mother, who modeled docility. Deep down, cholerics want to do the right thing and do not wish to offend God.

Of course, it's not always expedient or prudent to launch into long explanations. When your child is in danger or the situation is very serious, you can't waste any time. But don't resort to "Because I said so" if you're simply tired. Good reasons will almost always persuade a choleric — even a very stubborn one.[7] Through reason and supernatural motives, he can be persuaded to *change his own mind*, even if he doesn't willingly conform to yours.

The great Catholic psychiatrist Rudolf Allers, who studied under Sigmund Freud, discussed the importance of reason — especially when dealing with adolescents. But his advice is particularly relevant for parents of cholerics, no matter what their age, because reason weighs heavily with the choleric temperament. Allers writes about the adolescent (but we can easily substitute the choleric child): "If an appeal is made to his own independent reasoning, he may be brought to see the necessity of authority in general and of parental authority in particular."[8]

Every child needs to grow gradually in self-mastery and individuation, fundamental aspects of human development, and expressions of free will.[9] Overbearing and controlling parenting is never optimal, and it is more likely to provoke the choleric child to angry rebellion than any other temperament.[10]

## Cooling Off

The choleric child has a naturally strong sense of self, which is often manifested in stubbornness and pride. As a parent, you may sometimes react in frustration, wanting to break his will or mete out some severe punishment in order to bring him down a notch and make him more docile. But even Father Hock back in the early 1930s recognized that much care must be taken not to cause the choleric to become hardened and embittered by harsh and punitive discipline:

> [B]y hard, proud treatment the choleric is not improved, but embittered and hardened; whereas even a very proud choleric can easily be influenced by reasonable suggestions and supernatural motives ... it is absolutely necessary to remain calm and to allow the choleric to "cool off" and then to persuade him to accept guidance in order to correct his faults....[11]

We sometimes forget the importance of this cooling-off period with our own choleric. Once, Art became very upset when he found a rather crude expression written on sixteen-year-old Lucy's Facebook page. "I didn't write it!" Lucy insisted angrily. "Then why is it on your page?" Art demanded. Lucy stormed off, insulted, and refused to apologize for her disrespectful response. We later discovered that, indeed, she had not written anything inappropriate on her page but instead had been "tagged" in someone else's comment. When Laraine talked with Lucy much later and asked her why she didn't just apologize to her dad for flying off the handle or why, at least, she couldn't have *calmly* explained what happened, she replied: "I *couldn't* react calmly; I *had* to argue because it was *not true!*"

Our phlegmatic would have calmly explained the situation or would even have apologized for the appearance of wrongdoing. Our melancholic would have rationally explained (in great detail) how such a comment could have appeared on her Facebook page (*if* it had even happened at all!). But our choleric struggles to bring her strong reactions under control. Choleric children need to learn calming techniques (counting to ten before responding, taking deep breaths) and how to respond respectfully, even when they disagree or feel they have been unjustly accused.

When the parent reacts calmly, it shows the child that reason — not passion — reigns in the family; it helps us model for our children how to manage and regulate our passions. Father Hock points out that after remaining calm and allowing the choleric to cool off, parents can then "persuade him to accept guidance in order to correct his faults and bring out the good in him."[12]

When a parent deals with a choleric in anger, resorting to ever-escalating punishments, the choleric may not learn his lesson, nor will his inner spirit be changed. He can outlast you and remain obstinately committed to his position. We know one parent who has taken away privileges and has sent the determined choleric to time-out for longer and longer periods until the child was almost perpetually grounded and had no privileges left. This is only likely to harden the choleric's heart. Rather, what is needed is to touch his heart and help him to see the error of his ways through calm, objective discussions when the mood is peaceful and the child is receptive.

## *The Path to Prudence*

A choleric will mature in grace and wisdom when he has been convinced — by reason and supernatural motives — to choose the right path. If you simply force him to abide by your rules, he is more likely to become embittered and hardened.[13] Giving the reasons behind the rules and directions is one way to teach children to make their own good decisions. Learning how to make good decisions is the first step in learning the virtue of prudence, or right reason, which is the basis of a moral life. Of course, there are many occasions when it is perfectly appropriate to say "Because I said so!" but parents should seek out as many opportunities as possible to give their children good reasons for what they are asking. This helps children understand that parents and all appropriate authorities, including God and the Church, provide rules not based on autocratic despotism or whimsy but rather for good reason.

Parents need to help their choleric children choose the *right* goal. Enthusiasm and tenacity in pursuing their objective is admirable, but when the goal is wrong or immoral, the results can be seriously destructive. As Scripture says, "Train up a child in the way he should go, and when he is old he will not depart from it" (Proverbs 22:6).

■ ■ ■

### Discipline for Cholerics

a.  Punishment (grounding, taking away privileges) is not always effective: cholerics can outlast you. They are strong-willed and often dig in deeper. Allowing them to suffer natural consequences is often more effective.

b.  Allow a cooling-off period (for both you and your choleric) before showing them, in a calm, objective manner, what they did wrong.

c.  Use reason and appeal to supernatural motives.

■ ■ ■

Once directed on the right path, the choleric child can serve Christ expansively and with cheerful vigor. Simcha's little toddler (the one who bluntly referred to her mama's fat bottom) thought first to share her ice chips with her siblings when she was in the hospital after a serious accident. Seven-year-old Grace ("You need to dial 'one' ") offered her birthday presents to the poor children of Manassas, Virginia, who had none.

■ ■ ■

### Keys to the Choleric Child

•   Hard-wired to debate, quick temper. Help him fight the right fight.
•   Strong will: guide his will to accomplish the good.
•   Needs to have his accomplishments acknowledged.
•   Needs rational arguments and reasons.
•   Needs to have sense of control: give him age-appropriate choices.

■ ■ ■

# CHAPTER 3

# Your Moody
# Melancholic Moppet

*"I might have known," said Eeyore. "After all, one can't
complain. I have my friends. Somebody spoke to me only
yesterday. And was it last week or the week before that
Rabbit bumped into me and said 'Bother!' The Social Round.
Always something going on."*
A. A. MILNE, WINNIE-THE-POOH

She twirls dreamily, oblivious of the noisy preschool children romping rowdily around her; she is Clara from *The
Nutcracker*. She rarely joins a big crowd and would rather play
an imaginative, quiet game with one other girl or listen with
large eyes as the teacher reads a story. This is your sweet melancholic child.

## Characteristics of the
## Melancholic Child

Ancient Greeks, who classified everything according to the
four elements, thought the melancholic was cool, dark earth.
Melancholics are mysterious as a smooth stone on the sand
—impenetrable, dark, pressing into the ground — concealing beneath its surface something precious. Melancholics are
deep, serious, and idealistic.

**Still Waters:** Melancholic children may be described as having an "old soul." They love their friends dearly, yet they are quite comfortable alone — reading, playing, drawing, imagining. They may seem a bit different from the average child: more artistic, sensitive, gentle, or shy. Their reactions are slow to appear, yet deeply felt. They are keenly aware of (and most comfortable with) their internal world of thoughts and feelings, which sets them apart from an easy interaction with the external, social world. This cautious, idealistic child doesn't easily blend in with the rough-and-tumble childhood world.

Melancholics like to read, draw, daydream, or watch others at play, and they require more time than other children to feel comfortable enough to join in with a game or an activity. Because of their more acute sensitivities and internal focus, they might seem timid, daydreamy, or aloof: blood in the water for the sharks. Many times the melancholic child is the victim of bullies, childish tricks, or simply being left out.

**Low Threshold for Stimulation:** The baby or toddler that is slow to warm up, needs time to adjust to a new environment or food, gets overwrought after too much activity, cries when surprised, or hangs back at the sidelines before jumping into play may be a melancholic. Allow this child time to adjust to new situations, foods, places, or people. Be alert for signs of being overstimulated, such as long crying jags after a big day or throwing toys in frustration.

Melancholics love routine, order, and doing activities with Mom: Monday play group (with one friend), Tuesday story time at the library, Wednesday nature walk, and so on. Don't push this child to join a crowd or to be talkative before he is ready, because it is not a conscious decision that he is making;

he is intuitively compensating for his low threshold for stimulation. It is better to allow this child to watch the group for a while before jumping into play or to sit quietly with him, reading or talking to him, before you demand that he hold up his end of the conversation.

Don't leave this child to fend for himself with two or more playmates. Allow him to observe the play group before asking him to join in — and eventually you will enjoy all those parent-child activities that the independent sanguine or choleric child doesn't want to do with you. With time to adjust to new situations, gentle prodding, and positive experiences, the melancholic child will do fine.

**Unrealistic Expectations:** There is a saying that melancholics so long for heaven that everything on earth falls short. It explains their nobility of purpose, their tendency to perfectionism, and their unhappiness when things don't live up to their expectations.

When Michaela was five, her parents decided to give her swim lessons. She counted down the days with eager anticipation until finally the day of the first lesson arrived. She had a new suit, a special towel, and a swim bag. Her proud parents left her by the side of the pool in the care of the instructor and joined the other parents at the opposite end. Suddenly, a mournful wail rose like a firehouse siren from the small group of children awaiting instruction. It was Michaela's affronted voice: "This is not *at all* what I expected. Not ... at ... all!"

Michaela's mother, Robin, wondered, "What on earth could she have been expecting? Swim lessons are simple: pool, water, teacher." But Michaela had constructed something monumental and superlative in her mind, and the reality fell short. The tendency to live in one's head — a characteristic of melancholics — gives rise to all sorts of potentially unrealistic expectations: what school should be like, how friends should act, how siblings should behave, and so forth. One melancholic writer said about his childhood that although he didn't have an unhappy one, he didn't enjoy being a small child because of the "rank injustice" of never being listened to. This is not how things *ought* to be. At least not to a melancholic.

Once, when little Elijah was about three and a half, he refused to give his grandfather a hug good-bye. When asked why, he very somberly and seriously (wiping away tears and trying not to cry) responded: "I don't like it when you call me 'Bumper' because my name is Elijah."

**Time for Reflection Required:** Because they need time to process, melancholics don't always say or do exactly what is appropriate at the moment. They are more attuned to their inner thoughts and feelings and may miss the cue or respond to what they were thinking as opposed to what someone was asking. They may underreact or overreact — or they may not respond at all. Then they mull it over for a long time, perhaps even obsess a little about what they *should have* said or done. They replay the scene over and over in their minds: *Why didn't I say such-and-such when I had the chance?*

A young melancholic often lacks an easygoing humor in dealing with siblings and friends and takes teasing very hard. He may respond spitefully or with vengeance, thus alienating his siblings and friends even more by his overreaction. Taylor Swift is probably a melancholic. Her *Speak Now* album is all about things she thinks she should have said but didn't, and about wreaking vengeance upon those who have wronged her.

Sometimes parents think their melancholic is being deliberately disobedient or disrespectful when, in fact, the melancholic is still pondering what was asked of him or simply didn't hear his parents call him for dinner because he was daydreaming. Or he may miss the main point of the directive because he was so focused on a minor detail. These are not deliberate offenses, and parents should be gentle when helping their melancholic learn how to behave in such situations.

Their delayed response or hesitancy to react can create some problems for young melancholics: not raising their hand in class, not being picked for the game, waiting too long to join in a fun activity, failing to defend themselves, missing out on social opportunities, not going to the party, skipping tryouts for the team, staying home.

**Highly Sensitive:** A few years ago our daughter's high school staged the musical *Beauty and the Beast*. Art happened to come late to the matinee performance, and as he entered the lobby he saw a small group of children crying uncontrollably in the foyer — they were so frightened by the Beast that their parents had to take them out of the auditorium. Inside, there were many other children who were excited, nervous, or even smiling and cheering when they saw the scary Beast. Why were some four-, five-, and six-year-olds having a great time watching the show and another group of the same-age children demanding to leave? Most likely, the crying children in the lobby were highly sensitive melancholics.

**Idealistic:** Justice, noble ideals, and a longing for eternity mark this temperament. The young melancholic is easily drawn to prayer since reflection and the interior life come naturally to him. Solitude refreshes and restores the introverted melancholic, especially after a busy day at school or in social activities. Unlike the extraverted sanguine, who is easily bored and constantly in search of new activities and distractions, the melancholic will find himself energized by quiet, reflective time spent alone or with one other close friend. In fact, he needs this time alone or in a quiet place to recharge his batteries.

The female melancholic loves reading, romance, classic movies, sewing, art, and beauty. The male melancholic likes music, reading, structured events, clear lines of authority, time alone, and headphones. They both have the patience and eye for detail necessary for sewing or craft projects, design, woodworking, car repair, and other intricate work. A melancholic is a faithful, sensitive, trustworthy friend. He will listen with a sympathetic ear, rarely interrupting to tell his own story, and will provide empathic counsel when asked. Your melancholic child is your future artist, counselor, nurse, CPA, writer, priest, or religious.

## Inner Enthusiasm

Laraine presented the concept of temperaments to a class of twelve-year-old girls. To help the girls identify their own temperaments, she contrasted the melancholic with the opposite temperament, the sanguine: where the melancholic is serious, quiet, rarely speaking up in class, the sanguine is always talking, enthusiastic, boisterous. One clearly melancholic girl, who had thus far not raised her hand to speak and had observed the proceedings with wide, soulful eyes, timidly raised her hand. "What if," she whispered, "you're enthusiastic — on the inside?"

This captures melancholics: they want to talk, they love their friends, and they're enthusiastic, on the inside — or only with very close friends and family. Melancholics are introverts, but this does not mean simply that they are shy. Rather, it means they gain energy from their interior life; they are reserved and slow to warm up in social situations; they are more comfortable with their thoughts and their ideas; they are happy to socialize, especially with close friends and family, but it takes a toll.

When they grow older and more mature, they will become quite self-possessed and socially adept with the encouragement of their parents and teachers. They may appear cool and sophisticated with an aura of regality, like Grace Kelly or Cary Grant. They may even enjoy performing or speaking in front of audiences, provided there is a clear script or structure. But always, they are most comfortable in their interior world, and their preference is introversion.

## Learning Style, School, and the Melancholic Child

The melancholic child may appear to be distracted in school or in unfamiliar social situations. He is not actually distracted in the way a sanguine tends to be; in fact, the melancholic child is usually quite attentive to his teacher. If, however, there is a great deal of noise or confusion in the classroom, it may be overwhelming for the sensitive melancholic, who will then turn inward, attending to his own thoughts and trying to block out what he perceives as adverse stimuli.

In class, he will prefer not to raise his hand to ask a question, would rather not answer a question for fear of getting something wrong, and will often perceive the injustices of other children. He may turn too often to his parent to rescue him (unlike the choleric, who will go to battle in a heartbeat) and may become known as a tattletale or whistle-blower. If he has a strong-willed friend, the melancholic is likely to become his Sancho Panza, Robin, or Tonto — the ever-present sidekick. He may latch on to him, remain in his shadow, and imitate (even serve) the stronger child. The stronger friend provides the benefit of entrée into society, but the faithful melancholic child is always in danger of being cast aside or suffering at the hands of the more aggressive partner.

Because he has a tendency to internalize slight insults and worry about things he should have said or done, the melancholic may blow insignificant events out of proportion: the teacher *might* call on him, a child laughed at him, he dropped the ball during recess, and so forth. He ruminates over these events and, feeling them so deeply, develops stomachaches or headaches that prevent him from going to school. He prefers staying home anyway: sleeping in, reading, taking his time, spending time with Mom, daydreaming.

Parents should be attentive to their melancholics' deep feelings and sensitivities, but they should also remain firm when necessary. Yelling at them to finish their homework, rushing them to many after-school activities, or refusing to allow them to stay home when they are exhausted only adds to their anxiety. On the other hand, you don't want your melancholic to avoid responsibilities or miss important occasions, so you want to figure out what is bothering him and offer support and encouragement, without over-coddling.

## A Nurturing Environment

Melancholics will do best when the learning environment is quiet, structured, and nurturing. If they feel they are being judged harshly or are commanded to perform in front of the group (for example, being forced to speak extemporaneously), they might become too anxious to perform well. They relate well to teachers, especially when the teacher is nurturing and encouraging.

Our melancholic always excelled at schoolwork once she was older, but as a first-grader the chaotic modern-day style of the classroom overloaded her senses. She would get stomach-aches and feel stressed out by all the noise and chaos around her. We ended up homeschooling her through elementary school, but we can envision a classroom that would have been well suited to the needs of our melancholic child: small class size, low student-teacher ratio, orderly environment, nurturing teachers, quiet or music-filled space with plenty of artistic outlets and hands-on science projects. In fact, this was the way her grandmother, also an artistic melancholic, experienced elementary school.

Melancholics appreciate having quiet, cooperative learning environments with flexibility in which to express their artistic natures. They prefer controlling their own pace, allowing plenty of time to accomplish their tasks to their satisfaction without feeling pressured by deadlines or other students. The melancholic child will want to have plenty of time to think through the entire task before beginning, time to create that "perfect" little storybook, and time to solve her math problems or complete an essay. If you rush her, she may panic and throw something together that ultimately makes her feel unhappy.

A melancholic will strive to perform well in a class whether or not she feels the teacher likes her, unlike the sanguine, who might stop trying in a similar situation. Nonetheless, the melancholic may become deeply discouraged in such a case. When her teacher is nurturing, encouraging, and appreciative of the unique gifts of the melancholic, she will blossom.

Melancholics need downtime in which to decompress after a long school day — time for daydreaming, drawing, or playing imaginatively, rather than immediately jumping into homework, after-school activities, or more stressful situations. Melancholics take quite well to homeschooling, but they will need a little push to extend themselves outside their comfort zone.

■ ■ ■

### Melancholic Difficulties

- *Slow to initiate*
- *Prone to worry*
- *Negative outlook*
- *Lack of confidence*

■ ■ ■

## ENCOURAGING THE MELANCHOLIC CHILD

**"Just Do It" Doesn't Do It:** The melancholic, so prone to worry and discouragement, often needs a little kick start from parents, a good friend, or an older sibling when initiating a new activity or project. Your job as a parent is to *actively* encourage and support him. Melancholics do not respond to "Just do it!" If anything, this paralyzes them. They hesitate, wanting to do it just right, but they may never take those first steps. Melancholics live in the future and in the past, so they will worry about what they did wrong last time and foresee all sorts of difficulties in the future.

Melancholics would rather do nothing than join the new club, try out for the play, meet the new neighbors, or change majors. They need supportive parents to walk them into the classroom to meet the new teacher, hold their arms while swinging the bat, coach their first basketball team, give them some conversation starters, drive them to their first job interview, help them fill out college applications and pack for college, and hear them out when they are especially upset or worried.

As an undergraduate, our melancholic daughter got a job working at the fitness center on campus. The job was perfect: she could read a book or study as she checked IDs of the students who were coming to work out. She had had the job for about six months when we received a phone call one evening.

"Mom, I've been thinking about something, and I have a great idea!"

"What's your idea, Lianna?" Laraine asked.

"I'm thinking about *working out!*" she exclaimed.

A melancholic will *think* about working out for half a year!

**Planning and More Planning:** Melancholics may spend too much time on planning and preparing, and too little time putting their plans into action. When our melancholic was about eight years old, her favorite pastime was to rearrange our garage with a friend; they would set it up to look exactly like a store. This involved hours of rearranging, sweeping, organizing, and creating the interior of a store. By the time they were finished, it would be dark and time for the girls to go to bed. This didn't bother them at all. They would begin all over again the next day.

This tendency to plan and prepare continues into adulthood: the melancholic is the one who makes lists, plans strategies, makes sure the route is optimal (our melancholic planned our drive across the country — avoiding toll roads and identifying scenic spots), compares prices, follows the instructions, and reads the fine print.

It is sometimes difficult for melancholics to bring others aboard a project because they don't know how to convey enthusiasm for it, not because they lack that enthusiasm inside themselves. Sometimes, the melancholic just needs to vent about all that is wrong in her life. Parents might conclude that because their melancholic complains a lot, she must hate school or the job or the teacher. But complaining comes easily to melancholics, and it doesn't necessarily mean they want to quit their jobs or change schools. It usually means they want some empathy and understanding or support from their parents, but they don't know how to ask.

## Melancholics and New Situations

When faced with a stressful situation, the melancholic may want to avoid it altogether or think that what he needs is *more* sleep, *more* time to prepare, *more* analysis. But this can result in a cycle of lengthy deliberation in which he gets even more discouraged and stressed out. As our melancholic daughter faced a looming, seemingly impossible deadline to complete her dissertation, we would call to remind her to get started chipping away at it. "I don't want to talk about it," she would grumble. Melancholics may procrastinate because they fear that initial jump into the unknown or because they overthink simple decisions to the point of being paralyzed: *If I ask for help in chemistry, will the teacher think I am stupid? What if she is angry because I am interrupting her? Should I just send an email?*

If the anxiety is extreme, the melancholic may need professional help, perhaps cognitive behavior therapy or biofeedback. It is best to help him learn some stress-reduction techniques while young, for research indicates that if left unchecked, it can lead to depression and other disorders.[1] Parents can help their melancholic child get started by sitting with him, talking through some of the potential obstacles, and lending a supportive and encouraging ear. Once melancholics actually begin a project, they are supremely capable of self-denial, of being long-suffering, and of persevering through hell and high water.

Parents sometimes think the best way to introduce something potentially difficult, such as swim lessons or a move, is to spring it on children so that they don't have time to get upset. In fact, this approach does not work at all for melancholics. Remember, they are orderly, organized, and sequential — surprises don't work for them. Your melancholic is likely to complain, object, or cry, but these are his ways of working through the fear of change. Tell him in advance and discuss his fears: what is the worst that could happen? Role-play some ways of dealing with it, and give him time to process the new idea or plan. Firm, loving support is needed.

If something interpersonal is looming on the horizon — say, the homecoming dance, an invitation to a party, tryouts for the school play or the basketball team — the melancholic will stress about it. He might rationalize why it would be better to stay home, back out, or study. If he misses out on too many of the fun but anxiety-producing events — like parties, school dances, school plays, and musicals — he may become isolated and alone, reinforcing his anxiety about social situations rather than gradually overcoming them and growing in confidence.

Melancholics tend to be less physically vigorous than most people of other temperaments. While the choleric abounds in energetic purpose and the sanguine happily flits from activity to activity (while the phlegmatic chills on the couch), the melancholic is easily tired and is prone to small illnesses that sap his energy. The melancholic may require more sleep, yet his sleep may be interrupted by nighttime anxiety. The fairy tale "The Princess and the Pea" must have been about a melancholic! Nonetheless, consistent exercise and healthful eating habits will help your melancholic handle stress and maintain a healthy outlook on life.

## Disciplining the Melancholic Child

Harsh or punitive parenting may negatively affect the melancholic more than children of other temperaments: cholerics will rebel in anger, sanguines will immediately feel hurt and betrayed (yet are readily able to forgive), and phlegmatics' implacable calm will soon reappear. But melancholics will internalize the hurt, blame themselves, and hold on to the painful feelings for a long, long time. Excessive criticism can even cause a child to become *more* anxious — especially if he is, by temperament, predisposed to anxiety.[2]

■ ■ ■

*Instead of "Get your butt in gear!" try this: "What can I do to help you get started?"*

■ ■ ■

In fact, harsh or controlling parenting has been found to increase certain emotional disorders in children, potentially causing not only anxiety but social phobias and panic attacks.[3] Imagine a perfectionist melancholic parent exerting pressure on an equally perfectionist, self-critical, sensitive melancholic child. This is a recipe for anxiety disorders! There is no need to add harsh parental criticism to what the melancholic, in his insecurity and self-criticism, is already heaping upon himself. Better to give loving guidance and gentle reprimands.

Melancholics are sensitive, thin-skinned, and tend to overreact or underreact. You may be glancing at their hair and they will assume, "Oh, I look horrible!" Or you are tired and grumpy after a long day at work and you heave a heavy sigh — the melancholic thinks you are angry *at him*. They are overly sensitive to any perceived insult or glance askance, yet they themselves can be quite blunt and make hurtful comments without realizing it. In spite of their hypersensitivity, they don't realize how negative and critical they can be.

You might be tempted to yell or punish dramatically in order to get an immediate reaction or that outward expression of contrition for wrongdoing. You might also be tempted to reprimand your melancholic for his negativity and critical nature. When the melancholic child reacts in an over-the-top way to a mild parental rebuke or to minor indiscretions on the part of younger siblings, such as when they touch his things or move his stuff, you just want to yell "Lighten up!" or "Knock it off!" But remember, he is not intentionally being uncooperative. In fact, when your melancholic is being most disagreeable — grumpy, critical, complaining — that is when he *most* needs parental affection, words of encouragement, and praise for his efforts.

Keep in mind, however, that melancholics will not *ask for* the support they need as an outspoken choleric or a verbal sanguine might. Nevertheless, they do need it. They are more likely to grumble, complain, stress, implode, or run to their room than they are to ask you straightforwardly for your help. Give them the loving support they need anyway.

> When your melancholic is being most disagreeable — grumpy, critical, complaining — that is when he *most* needs parental affection, words of encouragement, and praise for his efforts.

In reprimanding a melancholic, it rarely works to say "Quit it!" or "What are you complaining about?" He may become even more embedded in his ways. When melancholics feel overwhelmed, they are inclined to overthink the problem or ruminate about it, which can exacerbate physical ailments. Studies have found that ruminating can fuel depression, impair problem solving, and drive away friends.

Because melancholics are so hard on themselves and so self-critical, harsh criticism only adds to their pain and rarely has a positive effect. It is far more effective to *reward* your melancholic when he does something right: catch him being kind to his annoying little sister or saying "I'm sorry" with sincerity. For example, "I noticed how sweet you've been with your little sister today. I know how annoying she can be sometimes, and it's beautiful the way you are showing such patience today."

Natural consequences and a gentle reprimand are usually sufficient punishment for bad behavior. For example, let's say an older melancholic sister asks her younger sister for help cleaning her room. But since the younger sister has been repeatedly subjected to complaints and criticism on previous occasions, the little sister says no. When the older child comes to you, complaining that her sister won't help, you might use this as a teachable moment. Ask her how she thinks the previous occasions went when they cleaned together: "Were you working as a team, or did you find a lot of fault with your younger sister?" Then figure out ways the two of them might cooperate better. A melancholic child will often need plenty of parental consults on how to be nicer, more cooperative, more appreciative, and flexible with siblings.

Even though the melancholic seems to dwell in the realm of the negative, this doesn't mean you should match his negativity with your own. In fact, the optimal ratio of positive to negative comments is five to one. For every five positive comments or gestures (a smile, a touch, a loving word), you may effectively utter a negative comment. Compliment your child over and over when she speaks out bravely, helps her younger siblings, or volunteers for a difficult project at school. You may think that abundant praise is over the top, but a melancholic needs plenty of reassurance and encouragement.

When the melancholic older sibling patiently plays with the younger one instead of yelling at him to get out of her room, when the melancholic student tackles a project without complaining and protesting that it is impossible, when the cautious melancholic spontaneously offers to help a neighbor — these are opportunities to be generous with praise. Even more than those of other temperaments, the melancholic will take your words (or your irritated glances) to heart. Spend time with your melancholic one-on-one. Have a late-night snack of milk and cookies just before bed or go out for dinner, just the two of you. Take these opportunities to praise his good, strong qualities and listen to his doubts and fears. Encourage him to step outside his comfort zone, make new friends, initiate a new project, or explore his environment.

As your melancholic works through the challenging teenage years, he will grow more adept at navigating social situations and stressful academic and work challenges. Many of the qualities that made life as a young child more demanding — his sensitivity, attention to detail, perseverance, responsibility, nobility of purpose — will serve him well as he becomes an accomplished and mature adult.

■ ■ ■

### Keys to the Melancholic Child

- *Avoid harsh or punitive discipline, as this may increase his anxiety.*
- *Be firm but gentle.*
- *First connect with empathy, and then ask for a change.*
- *Catch him being positive, helpful, and cooperative, and praise him for it.*
- *Use rewards and words of affirmation to direct the melancholic positively.*

■ ■ ■

# CHAPTER 4

# Your Spirited Sanguine Sprout

*"Tiggers never go on being Sad," explained Rabbit.*
*"They get over it with Astonishing Rapidity."*
A. A. Milne, *Winnie-the-Pooh*

The sanguine child comes into the world like a shooting star. Even as an infant, he seems to glow: "Here I am, world!" He is an enthusiastic learner, eagerly exploring and testing the limits of all boundaries. Your ebullient, charming, and above all *talkative* sanguine will give you and your family much joy — and a wealth of hands-on parenting experience.

## Characteristics of the Sanguine Child

According to the ancient Greek classification of everything according to elements, the sanguine was air: moving, changing, and blowing this way and then that. Keeping up with a sanguine's moods and attitudes is like riding a roller coaster: one moment up, the next moment down.

**Lively:** Sanguines are active babies, eager to explore and likely to protest being confined to car seats and any baby apparatus. Our sanguine, Sam, was somewhat mollified by the mobility of the baby backpack carrier — at least he could see out — but was only truly content once he could toddle around on his own power. He started speaking early, at ten months, and would surprise passersby as he called out "Hi" from his baby stroller.

**Expressive:** The sanguine child has an expressive, alert, mobile face that matches his temperament. Your melancholic child will have a dreamy, unfocused, thoughtful, perhaps pensive, gaze; the phlegmatic will appear placid and agreeable; and a choleric child looks pugnacious and ready to rumble. But the sanguine child is highly emotive and very *expressive*: looking around, smiling, waving to friends, talking, laughing, and generally very open and outwardly interested. This is true of sanguine adults as well. (Laraine often enjoys scanning the congregation before Mass to identify fellow sanguines: they are the ones looking around, smiling, nodding hello. The melancholics are devoutly praying with their eyes closed.)

One of our favorite memories of our sanguine son as a toddler took place when he was two. We had taken Sam to daily Mass, and he was quite annoyed that we were spending a long time — to his two-year-old mind — chatting afterward. We were talking with Pat, an elderly gentleman who was trying to include Sam in the conversation. Uncharacteristically silent, Sam fixed a wordless glare on our friend. Finally Pat said, "Sam, why aren't you answering my questions?"

"Don't you see my eyes?" demanded Sam.

**Mercurial:** The sanguine is happy and chatting one moment, sad and tearful the next. One day he wants to be an NBA basketball star and the next he wants to be a Nobel Prize-winning journalist. Parents should be aware that he may come running home in tears after playing with a friend, and two minutes later all will be forgotten. Negative moods rarely last long, and he is very forgiving; soon, he will return to his typically sunny personality. His distractibility and changeable moods will continue well into high school and perhaps even beyond. We observed — and other parents of sanguines will testify to this — that as the sanguine grows older and more mature, he is capable of concealing and even overcoming his moods, and he may even become rather circumspect as he works through the stormy period of adolescence. But still, sanguines are known for their changeability. One sanguine college student asked her teacher if she could (again!) change the topic for her persuasive speech. The teacher responded, "I sure am glad I didn't bring you to Baskin-Robbin's thirty-one flavors!" Sanguines love to change hobbies, jobs, college majors, and even their college.

**Distractible:** Your busy sanguine is by nature easily distracted. Eager and enthusiastic at the outset, he then quickly loses interest and is on to another game, activity, or book. That's why helping the sanguine extend his attention span is important.

You can harness his enthusiasm and desire to please. Your sanguine loves doing things *for you*, unlike the choleric, who enjoys the *task itself*, or the melancholic, who wants to complete the task *well*. By tapping into this motivating force, parents can help the sanguine strengthen his will and increase his attention span. Ask him to help you around the house or yard with small but interesting or fun jobs, emphasizing *completion*: putting away his toys, checking the mailbox, setting the table, or following a recipe. First, you work on completing the task; later you can help him attend to detail. He is willing to take direction as long as the task doesn't become overly tedious or painstaking, and he is rarely directly defiant or obstinate unless he is also partly choleric.

## LEARNING STYLE, SCHOOL, AND THE SANGUINE CHILD

Our sanguine friend Beth recalls her earliest memory of grade school. She looked around the room at her fellow classmates and wondered, "Why are they all looking straight ahead at the teacher or else down at their desks?" The people-loving, distractible sanguine is looking *everywhere else* — anywhere other than where she ought to be looking.

### Keeping It Active

At school, your sanguine child is likely to be the class clown or the one who gets in trouble for talking, interrupting, and forgetting her homework. With their energetic and easily distractible natures (remember, it's the way they are wired; they're not willfully inattentive or disruptive), sanguines learn more easily through hands-on activities engaging all their senses. They don't like to sit passively in their seat; they would rather be doing jumping jacks while learning the multiplication tables or singing a song with the names of all the state capitals. They need activity, flexibility, and exciting, interactive, or storytelling presentations. They learn abstract or difficult concepts best when they can relate them somehow to their own personal experience.

If you are homeschooling, be aware that sanguines will enjoy art projects, kitchen science projects, field trips, going to the library for story hour, supermarket trips for applied math, museums, firehouses, and so on. Make learning fun. When you are teaching an abstract concept, help your sanguine connect to it by relating it to a familiar movie or story or to someone he knows. Help him break down a big project into smaller, more manageable portions, and then give gentle reminders; otherwise he will be sorely tempted to leave everything until the last minute!

Sitting still and reading is not much fun at first, especially for a sanguine boy. Our sanguine developed his love for reading by spending time with the newspaper, particularly the sports section, starting when he was eight. He graduated from the newspaper to short books. The key was capturing his interest: sports, mysteries, and literature. By the time he was in high school, he was reading Kierkegaard and Dostoyevsky. His sanguine temperament reveals itself in the high library fines he gets for forgetting to return his books. With typical sanguine charm, however, he also is quite adept at talking his library fines down.

## Getting It Organized

Sanguine kids need help with organization and planning. As soon as your sanguine gets home from school, ask him what is due the next day. Be specific. In elementary school, our sanguine used to come home claiming he had no homework. We discovered that he had defined homework so narrowly that projects, papers, and tests were not included. We had to ask specifically whether he had anything that was either due the next day or that he had to study in preparation for a test. And even then, we had to run through the list of subjects as a reminder.

Also check what might be on the horizon since sanguines often need help in planning ahead. Give him a hand in organizing his books and folders in a fun way, perhaps using color coding or letting him choose his own folders and binders to keep his subjects organized. Show him how to create a system for remembering what he needs to bring to school the next morning and have him set out everything — every item of clothing, his backpack, and whatever else he needs — the night before. You might think this is a lot of trouble to go through for one child, but the advance preparation, with you involved, is worth it. It will save you mornings of running around the house looking for that matching sock, the sports bag, the essay left on the printer, the missing history book, or the permission form he forgot to get signed. And it will demonstrate for him the importance of planning and organization.

When your sanguine child is just starting school, you may have to help him discover what inspires him to be organized and to study hard: index cards with color-coded pens for memorizing, a planner with inspirational or funny quotes, special notebooks, and so forth. Work with him to develop a system. Don't just yell, "Why can't you remember anything?" when he comes home from school without his math book.

Sanguines often need a parent's guidance in breaking a big project down into manageable portions — otherwise they might delay getting started. When you need to give him constructive criticism, remember first to praise his efforts — which in his mind were monumental — and then gently but firmly walk him through what he could have done better in order to be more successful. If he is having trouble getting started on a project or studying for a big exam, sit down together for a "powwow" or planning session.

If you are a sanguine parent raising a sanguine child and you are homeschooling — watch out! This is a recipe for plenty of fun, but possibly not as much schoolwork as you might have hoped. A sanguine homeschooling household is more likely to be seen out on field trips to the planetarium or museum, baking chocolate-chip cookies for science class, at the playground for P.E., and watching *The Price Is Right* for math.

The sanguine enjoys flexibility and freedom so much that he may resist structure and discipline, yet this is just what he needs. If you are homeschooling a young sanguine, it helps to firmly enforce order and structure: although flexibility is one of the main strengths of a home school, it can become a weakness for the sanguine child, who naturally makes the most of this perk. Clear rules and objective measures of success are critical for the sanguine.

You can be flexible, however, in presenting interesting subjects, exploring creative ways to enliven the duller subjects, and allowing your sanguine to pursue those that pique his interest. If you offer relatively short-term projects, but emphasize completion, your sanguine will learn to develop perseverance. Soon, he will discover those subjects that he is most interested in and will want to pursue them in greater depth.

## Making It Personal

A sanguine will learn most readily when his teachers are animated, engaging, and connecting with their students through personal anecdotes. A personal connection is vital, but a sanguine finds it difficult to establish a personal connection when the teacher (or coach, pastor, parents, or boss) is cold, impersonal, or dour.

The sanguine needs to feel appreciated by his leaders and mentors. Many times our sanguine son would struggle to do well in a class where, despite his own talent in the given subject, he felt the teacher didn't like him. When a sanguine thinks that someone doesn't like him, he is likely to become discouraged and may not perform up to par. The problem is, a sanguine also has an uncanny knack for annoying teachers, especially if the teacher is an organized, detail-oriented, serious melancholic. When faced with the impulsive, attention-getting antics of the fun-loving and scatterbrained sanguine — well, you have trouble ahead.

## THE SOCIAL LIFE OF SANGUINES

When Sam was in the fifth grade (we were homeschooling), he met his neighborhood friends at the bus stop every day after school and walked them home. It was the highlight of his day. As the time approached, his eyes would light up with sheer joy at the prospect of seeing his buddies come home from school. He begged to attend school so that he could ride the bus, too. We let him go to school in the sixth grade, but we made sure he understood that we expected hard work and good grades. He performed extremely well. In fact, he put in far greater effort than he ever had for our home school. We believe that his good performance had something to do with the fact that we were building on his natural strength of sociability, instead of forcing him to do without it.

The lack of opportunities to socialize is a drawback for a sanguine. Friends are vitally important to this extraverted child, and typically he wants lots of them. Allow your sanguine to make friends — *good* friends who exhibit moral behavior and whose parents share critical values with you. True friendship combines charity and goodwill, and it helps children grow in virtue as well as maturity. As a parent, you can help your sanguine learn to set limits and to make wise judgments about friends and activities.

Parents can sometimes feel overwhelmed by this child's big, vocal personality. At times, when you are feeling beleaguered by that tenth request to go see a movie, or the number of friends he continually invites to spend the night, or the parties he engineers, remind yourself that at least he freely shares his desires, his friends, and his interests with you. There may come a time when you will wish your kids were more expressive. Some children rarely reveal anything about what goes on inside — the characteristic phlegmatic "I don't know," for example — and as they enter adolescence they often go through a period when they are reluctant to share their thoughts and feelings. With your sanguine, you will be well aware!

Art once posed a question to our two boys: "What would you do if you could have a day in New York City?" Our phlegmatic son said thoughtfully, "Hmmm, I don't know. Let me think about it." Our sanguine was bursting with ideas: "I'd go to a game at Yankee Stadium, take a walk in Central Park, visit the Nike store and Times Square.... Oh, and we'd go out to eat at Alfredo's and maybe hit Elaine's and hear Woody Allen play clarinet!"

When our sanguine was only eight years old, he asked, "Why do my friends always want to have their birthday parties at Chuck E. Cheese's? I want a different kind of party — the kind where everyone is standing around talking and eating."

"Oh," we replied, "that's called a cocktail party!" Even in his young mind, that would be the ultimate. Sanguines will plan menus for the Super Bowl party, pick out movies for a home movie night, and defend family traditions. On one occasion, Art took Sam out on a special movie night, just the two of them. Sam became visibly saddened as Dad began criticizing the movie. He not only wanted to see the movie with Dad, but he wanted Dad to enjoy it as much as he did. A sanguine child not only wants to see a movie, watch the game, or go out to eat — he wants everyone to enjoy the movie, the game, and the dinner. Sanguines are hosts, not just participants.

## DISCIPLINING THE SANGUINE CHILD

Your irrepressible sanguine will inevitably test your parenting patience. Sanguines rarely intend to annoy or consciously rebel; they simply cannot contain their enthusiasm for new adventures, new friends, new fashions, or new toys. Parents can become wearied by the sanguine's incessant talking and his many needs — which he readily expresses: "When are we going Christmas shopping? ... Can I get an Xbox? ... I really need a new bike! ... I don't have anything to wear! ... All my friends are getting skateboards! ... Can I sleep over again this weekend? ... Let's go out for hot wings and watch the playoffs! ... Everyone is going to Beach Week! ... Are we taking a family vacation this year? ... I need a car!" And on and on.

### Set Limits and Expectations Ahead of Time

In order to corral and direct the sanguine's enthusiasms, parents must be clear and decisive about rules, limits, and expectations *ahead of* time. Let your sanguine know that there is a limit to the Christmas budget, that you expect him home no later than midnight, that you want him to call as soon as he arrives at his friend's house, and that he must maintain a specified GPA in order to keep his driver's license. You can invite your sanguine to be a part of the decision making — this encourages buy-in — but make it clear that ultimately you are in charge. Parents can be clear about limits and expectations without being repressive or overbearing.

Of course, if you are indecisive about your rules, he may take advantage of you. When you say, "I'll think about it," your sanguine will often take this as "Yes." Without firm structure and guidance, sanguines tend to push the limits.

As with all your children, but especially with your sanguine child, make sure you know who his friends are, what he is watching on television, and where he is. Help him stay on task with his academics: sanguines tend to stop studying the moment they *feel* they have put in enough time, unlike the melancholic student, who will not stop until he has mastered the material. Even when you insist that he study more, a sanguine's natural optimism convinces him that "I totally own this subject! I don't need to study any longer." He will learn through trial and error that discipline and hard work are necessary ingredients for academic success. And you will have to check up on him rather than take his word that assignments have been completed.

> Be forewarned, however: the sanguine temperament is the most likely to learn from experience — in other words, the hard way — and the least likely to simply abide by the rules or take a parent's advice at face value.

### Learning the Hard Way

Sanguines are impulsive and don't always reflect on whether their impulsive choice is a good or bad one. They have to be cautioned not to make rash decisions. They also find it difficult to resist temptation, yet are genuinely remorseful when they fall. One mom of a sanguine told us that her college-age son had been drinking heavily one evening and felt so sorry about it that he turned himself in to the campus police! She received a call the next morning from the dean of students, who said that her son would not be charged with anything because he had never committed any infractions before and was a great kid. The dean thought he had learned his lesson.

Be forewarned, however: the sanguine temperament is the most likely to learn from experience — in other words, the hard way — and the least likely to simply abide by the rules or take a parent's advice at face value. For example, our sanguine son parked his car in the tow-away zone while visiting his brother at college. Sam said to himself, "They don't really enforce these signs; I'm just going to be here for a couple of hours." Naturally, he returned to find his car towed away, to the tune of $150. He had to learn through experience.

■■■

*Instead of "Stop fooling around and do your homework!" try this: "Let's do some Zumba, and then you can start your homework."*

■■■

## Staying on Task

Without guidance and clear structure, distractible sanguines are prone to taking the path of least resistance — which, coincidentally, is usually the path of most fun. You can capitalize on this inclination by including an element of play or fun when your sanguine needs to accomplish an important task or when you want to instill a particular value. For example, when you want your young sanguine to go to confession, don't try to inspire him with "You have been really bad lately." Try an upbeat "You will feel so great after confession! And then we'll go out for ice cream to celebrate our new state of grace!"

Whether the occasion calls for an aspect of fun or not, when you give your sanguine a task (such as cleaning her room), don't assume she can go off and emerge an hour later with mission accomplished, as a melancholic would. It's more likely that the sanguine got distracted and began playing with her Polly Pockets. Instead, check on her every fifteen minutes or so, and when she has completed half the task, give her a break as a small reward.

Finally, the connectedness of the media age presents a particular challenge for the sanguine child. Kids today spend more time on their cell phones and on the Internet each day than with their family or on schoolwork.[1] The temptation to waste hours on Facebook, texting, or with other media is heightened for the distractible sanguine. He may be convinced that he is an expert multitasker, but research has proven that nobody can really effectively multitask. The sanguine will become even more disorganized and distracted than he already was. Setting strict limits on the use of media, as well as encouragement in pursuing his studies, along with recreational reading and sports, will keep your sanguine focused and healthy.

The increased demands of high school and young adulthood challenge your sanguine to become more organized, attentive, and persevering. On his own, he will begin to appreciate his parents' gentle insistence on these qualities. He will value his parents' help in encouraging him to develop the study and personal habits he needs to become a disciplined, mature individual.

■■■

### Keys to the Sanguine Child

- *Set clear expectations, rules, and limits ahead of time.*
- *Show appreciation for his friendliness, enthusiasm, and initiative. Reward difficult tasks with something fun (ice cream after confession, for example).*
- *Show interest in his friends, but encourage him to choose wisely.*
- *Don't take away his fun, but don't leave him entirely to his own devices.*
- *Provide structure and order.*
- *Monitor projects and tasks closely; walk him through a difficult task the first time around.*

■■■

# CHAPTER 5

# Your Peaceful
# Phlegmatic Progeny

*"It is more fun to talk with someone who doesn't use long,
difficult words but rather short, easy words like,
'What about lunch?' "*
A. A. MILNE, *WINNIE-THE-POOH*

Ah, the beauty of the phlegmatic child: quiet, easygoing, good-natured, cooperative. If this child is your first, know that you are blessed, but don't succumb to pride, thinking that you have superior parenting skills. These babies are just made that way.

And if you haven't yet had a phlegmatic child, keep on trying until you do!

## Characteristics of the Phlegmatic Child

In the ancient Greek elemental theory, the phlegmatic was water: calm, cool, and conforming to the shape of whatever vessel contains it. The phlegmatic goes with the flow.

**Placid:** As an infant, Ray, our phlegmatic, used to sit contentedly in his little baby seat, spitting up quietly and constantly, yet never making a fuss (today he would be diagnosed with acid reflux). Once we all left a neighborhood toy store, while Ray was still quietly lining up the Brio trains in a corner. (Of course, we immediately returned to fetch him!) Even as a toddler, there were no tantrums, no "terrible twos." His only vice was his Houdini-like talent to wriggle out of any car seat, no matter how securely we tied him in. He was a baby when we lived in Germany, and we can still remember our shock as we would glance back to see Ray standing up in triumph in his car seat, raising his little hands over his head in victory as we hurtled down the autobahn at breakneck speed. This was a foreshadowing of his love for roller coasters. Even the most thrilling ride seems to have no impact on his phlegmatic, unflappable calm.

The phlegmatic infant is the classic "easy" baby. He sleeps well, rarely cries, and doesn't make a fuss over his food. In a large and busy household, the phlegmatic baby is a true gift. He hardly ever throws a tantrum and is easily entertained. We have a photograph of our phlegmatic son at age five, dressed in leotard and tulle, obediently performing a pirouette under the demanding direction of his older sister for one of her many home performances of the *Nutcracker*. Cooperative, compliant, and agreeable — these are the hallmarks of the phlegmatic temperament.

**Can't We All Just Get Along?:** Phlegmatics are averse to conflict, especially interpersonal conflict. They want everyone to get along, to be as pleasant and peaceful as they are. On one occasion, Ray sat silently in the backseat of our minivan, while chaos erupted all around him. Siblings were arguing, parents were remonstrating, and the dog was barking. Finally, Ray heaved a big sigh: "Can everyone just, please, be quiet!"

In a large family, the phlegmatic can find his senses over-whelmed by his siblings (and sometimes his parents) angrily shouting or fighting. In these situations, a melancholic might have a vocal meltdown and run into his room, slamming the door, but the phlegmatic child will simply put up with it.

The peace-loving phlegmatic would rather sacrifice his own desires, agree to unreasonable demands — even take unjust punishment — to keep the peace. This is true even if it is *not* ultimately in his best interest. One day our phlegmatic son was feeling overwhelmed. His choleric mother was interrogating him about what colleges he was planning on applying to and demanding to know what steps he had taken thus far. Phlegmatic-melancholic Dad was gloomily lecturing on the Lack of Academic Motivation in the Youth of Today. Our son's shoulders slumped, and his eyes began drooping sadly. Suddenly he brightened up. "I know," he said. "You just make me a list of my top three schools, and I will apply to them!" Our son was willing to *abdicate his own choice* in order to please his parents, dispel the anxiety associated with contemplating an unknown and scary future, and avoid an onerous outlay of effort.

Phlegmatics love peace and harmony as much as their parents do, but this kind of peace was really just the absence of conflict resulting from the path of least resistance, rather than the fruit of choosing the right thing and taking principled action. So while it may be easier for parents to say, "Okay, I'll decide for you," the better choice is to help your phlegmatic look into the future — and into the depths of his own soul — and encourage him to find his passion.

One day your phlegmatic may become a diplomat, negotiating peace treaties with inscrutable calm. Or he might be a careful, meticulous engineer, whose methodical and precise calculations enable a soaring bridge to span an enormous chasm. Or he may become a calm and dedicated firefighter or soldier, whose courage and self-sacrifice save lives and serve the many.

**A Temperament of Few Words:** Although phlegmatics are usually outwardly agreeable, they are not always communicative. When our phlegmatic son was very young, we proudly — and anxiously — watched him swim his first one-hundred-meter butterfly at an invitational meet. We saw his coach calling him over to speak to him after the event. From a distance, we could see the coach earnestly gesticulating, demonstrating strokes, and putting an arm on our son's shoulder, while Ray dutifully nodded. Finally, when he came back to join us, we eagerly asked, "What did he tell you?"

"I don't know," said Ray.

We soon learned that this short phrase is a hallmark of phlegmatics, young and old alike. When a friend of ours quizzed her eleven-year-old son about his homework, her son assured her that he didn't have to study too much for his social-studies test because he had already studied during class. "Oh, what's the test on?" asked his mom.

"I don't know," replied phlegmatic Ryan.

Perhaps it takes too much energy to come up with a response, perhaps their reaction is merely delayed, or perhaps they are stalling in order to find out what answer will be most acceptable to the questioner. Or perhaps they're trying to nap. When he was older, in an effort to solve this mystery, we quizzed Ray. "When you say that you don't know, do you *really* mean 'I know — but I don't want to tell you' or perhaps 'I'm pondering very deep and difficult concepts that cannot be put into words at this moment'?"

"No," replied Ray affably. "I just don't know."

**You Decide:** "No, *you* decide." A phlegmatic will often defer decision making to others: "I don't care; whatever *you* want to do" is a common refrain. As youngsters, Ray and his equally phlegmatic friend Steve would call each other after school: "What do you want to do?" "I don't know, whatever *you* want." "No, no, you decide!" Phlegmatics don't really like to stick their neck out or endure the headache of deciding, or risk making the wrong choice. It's easier this way. As a parent, you might feel gratified that this child actually listens to you, takes your advice, or defers to your judgment. Nonetheless, he will need to learn to speak up, make up his own mind, and sometimes take a stand. This is an important part of growing up. Once a phlegmatic does make up his mind, he can stick to it with an iron will — all the while presenting an agreeable appearance of conformity because he doesn't like to disagree with you.

## LEARNING STYLE, SCHOOL, AND THE PHLEGMATIC CHILD

Phlegmatics are beloved by weary and beleaguered teachers everywhere. The phlegmatic child sits quietly at his desk, rarely disturbing his classmates, dutifully gazing in the direction of the teacher (if not actually taking notes), and politely answering questions (only when called on). He rarely disrupts the class and will not object to those rote-learning study sheets that he obediently fills out, and he is fine with parroting back on a test whatever the teacher said. He looks attentive, but his mind may be elsewhere. Teachers need to make sure that the phlegmatic actually understands the material and is actively engaged. The key is to challenge and engage the phlegmatic in the process of learning.

Ray once took a high school class where, as we later discovered, nothing was taught and the kids spent the hour tossing wads of paper into the wastebasket. Unfortunately, he never told anyone about this until it was too late. A phlegmatic rarely complains.

Phegmatics prefer structured classes that are organized, clear, specific, and orderly. They don't like it when teachers are vague, disorganized, or fail to give specific guidelines about what counts toward the grade. If they are only presented with the end goal, phlegmatics may need help in breaking it down into smaller portions with achievable benchmarks. Additional materials such as workbooks, tables and charts, concrete examples, sample tests, and templates will help the careful, detail-oriented phlegmatic to learn well.

In school, for example, the phlegmatic is not likely to stand out in the crowd — a teacher, coach, or even a scout leader may pass over this unassuming and soft-spoken personality. The choleric is aggressively debating, the sanguine is charming everyone, the melancholic is striving for perfection — but the phlegmatic may be overlooked.

Phlegmatics work well in groups or teams — they are excellent team players — and are extremely cooperative and hardworking. If the classroom is an aggressive dog-eat-dog environment, however, phlegmatics will feel insecure and may withdraw.

Phlegmatics often perform better in smaller classes or in schools where they are comfortable with their friends. In this supportive environment, they can develop public-speaking skills, do class reports and presentations, and take on leadership roles.

## The Underestimated Temperament

As you can surmise, the phlegmatic's placid, taciturn nature can have its own drawbacks. In school, for example, the phlegmatic is not likely to stand out in the crowd — a teacher, coach, or even a scout leader may pass over this unassuming and soft-spoken personality. The choleric is aggressively debating, the sanguine is charming everyone, the melancholic is striving for perfection — but the phlegmatic may be overlooked.

Even worse, because they tend to be somewhat passive and slow to react, phlegmatics are often accused of laziness or of lacking leadership skills (even Father Conrad Hock said as much[1]). But this is, in our view, a terrible mistake. Phlegmatics have a great capacity for leadership and for academic success, as is evident in their ability to work well with everyone (even those with difficult temperaments), their willingness to work hard, their levelheadedness under pressure, and their dedicated service to others.

In fact, the phlegmatic has many gifts that contribute to excellence in leadership. Perhaps their greatest gift, however, is their natural humility: the ability to ask for help and to seek guidance is a key quality in leaders. Our son graduated from a well-known engineering school, as an engineer, despite not being naturally gifted in math. But Ray was willing to ask for help, even though other students found this too embarrassing. In fact, he would go straight from class to meet with professors during office hours. He said that he knew he would have trouble with the homework, so why not just admit it and get help immediately, instead of wasting time.

This natural humility shapes the phlegmatic leadership style: phlegmatics are best described as "servant leaders," leading quietly but unmistakably by example and hard work, rather than with flamboyant words, charisma, or power. One phlegmatic teen we know had been repeatedly ignored and even rebuffed by her peers at school. She was soft-spoken, never flamboyant, and not given to the typical gossip teenage girls indulge in. Because she never bragged, few people realized that she was a star athlete. Yet on her swim team, she was recognized and respected by the other kids. They voted her team captain for her sincere hard work and dedication.

The trick, though, is to convince phlegmatics to take charge. Because they don't seek the limelight, most need a gentle push to accept leadership responsibilities — but once they've done so, they can thrive. You can help your phlegmatic grow in self-confidence and a sense of self-worth by encouraging him to seek out opportunities to serve others, to lead, and to excel. The best way to help your phlegmatic bloom is to be overtly appreciative and encouraging.

It is important to encourage your phlegmatic child to take on leadership roles in school and in other areas, not only as a way to help him develop self-confidence but also because at some point in our lives each one of us needs to step up and be a soldier for Christ. We will need to speak the truth even when it is uncomfortable, and we will need to serve the Church even when we don't feel like it.

## Disciplining the Phlegmatic Child

Parenting a phlegmatic child demands less of a parent in terms of discipline, and more in terms of motivating. As we have seen, the phlegmatic temperament is wonderfully docile and obedient. Phlegmatic children rarely push the envelope, test limits, or are willfully defiant. And they rarely require disciplining in the sense of stern consequences or punishments. In fact, Ray only once got into big trouble, and that was inadvertently. He was — phlegmatically — tagging along with some friends who had suggested a midnight excursion on the beach.

Again, phlegmatics don't purposefully or naturally seek out trouble, bad companions, or dangerous situations. They might accidentally find themselves in trouble by being too passive, by going along with the crowd, or by failing to do the right thing. So it is good for parents to warn their phlegmatic children that there can be sin in *omission* as well as commission.

■■■

*Instead of "Is there anything going on inside that head of yours?" Try this: "Let's go out for smoothies, and we can talk about what's going on at school."*

■■■

A phlegmatic teen we know got in trouble for cheating on a test. He had felt enormous pressure to achieve top grades, and he wasn't especially gifted in this particular subject. The pressure to perform outweighed his natural moral sense, and he succumbed to the temptation to cheat. But generally speaking, when a phlegmatic is raised in a strong Christian household, where morals are clearly taught, he will naturally want to

93

please his parents and conform to their moral standards and God's law.

The greater danger for phlegmatics is becoming apathetic, dull, and slothful. They are comfortable in the present and with the status quo. Because they are not naturally confident like cholerics, nor gunning for attention like sanguines, they can underestimate themselves and unwittingly set themselves up to be ignored by teachers and other adults. If they are not encouraged — with much loving praise — they might never find their own talents, strengths, and interests.

Worse, if they are ignored, nagged, or hounded, they may retreat into passive activities like video games or become terribly discouraged. It is our opinion that there are many phlegmatics who have never reached their potential because they have not been given the necessary encouragement. And when they are already struggling with school or a project, harsh judgments and intimidating lectures will not help them achieve that confidence they need to keep persevering.

Nagging, lecturing, and yelling will cause the sensitive phlegmatic to withdraw in discouragement. Instead, parents should encourage them with overt praise, practical assistance, and positive feedback. A gentle push or a reasonable suggestion will work wonders. When Ray was ten years old, for example, he was the second-fastest freestyler on his summer swim team. He was always forced to swim backstroke (which he hated) in the medley relays because Geoffrey was faster than he was. We told him, "Why don't you just beat Geoffrey and then *he* will have to swim backstroke?" "Oh, I couldn't do that!" replied Ray. "Why not?" we asked. So he dutifully tried — and succeeded! For the rest of the summer, Ray maintained the fastest freestyle time of his age group.

It is always helpful for parents to remind their phlegmatic of his strengths and his past successes. When Ray was heading off to college, we asked him what his greatest concern was. He said he wasn't sure he would be disciplined on his own. We reminded him of the many times he showed independent self-discipline as an athlete: "We never had to force you to get up early for swim practice; you just did that on your own." Ray replied, "You're right. I never thought of it that way!"

A parent's job is to help his or her children connect those dots, to encourage self-confidence and the feeling of competence that will ensure future success.

### Keys to the Phlegmatic Child

- *Engage him often, encouraging social and leadership skills.*
- *Praise him frequently for his cooperation, his good attitude, and his achievements.*
- *Don't ridicule, nag, or criticize harshly: help him build confidence and a sense of competence.*
- *Watch out for discouragement.*
- *Motivate; don't just legislate or take over for him.*

# CHAPTER 6

# WHAT'S *YOUR* TEMPERAMENT?

*Parents are ... the first heralds of the Gospel for their children.*
BLESSED JOHN PAUL II

We remember so vividly that day in 1984 when we drove away from the hospital with our newborn first child. As the tiny six-pounder lay slumped in the too-large car seat, we looked at each other and exclaimed, "How can they let us take her home?"

A parent's job can seem impossible: you are the protector, the guardian, the advocate, the loving teacher who must help each one of God's precious creations know, love, and serve God in this life and ultimately be happy with him in heaven. The family is the first place where children learn how to love. It is an "intimate community of life and love."[1] It is the first place children *experience* love: through the loving relationship of their parents, their parents' love for them, and the gift of their siblings. Children learn about God's love through their parents' example.

What a monumental, daunting task we parents have. And, for single parents, it can seem even more daunting![2] With God, however, all things are possible (Matthew 19:26).

## TWO SHIPS ON A TRUE COURSE

We like to think of parents as captains of two ships as they guide their family: leader*ship* and relation*ship*. Both are essential.

**Leadership:** Leadership means that we guide our children to Christ and the Church. We know that our family needs Christ in order to have the grace and strength to withstand temptation and to become beacons of light and truth in the world. Parents lead their families by modeling discipline, patience, self-sacrifice, humility, and prudence. These virtues will help your children avoid two of the most damaging and common cultural pitfalls: individualism and materialism.

**Relationship:** Most important, parents teach their children to love. In order to be strong leaders of their families, parents must be attentive to the quality of their relationship with their children. This includes listening empathically to hear their side of the story, apologizing when necessary, and being forgiving. This relationship is not a chummy buddy system that creates a culture of permissiveness and irrational feelings. It is, rather, the cultivation of an atmosphere of respect and affection so that the first ship, leadership, can effectively steam ahead. If you do not have a relationship with your kids, they may not listen to you once they are past the age of being controlled by you.

The choleric and melancholic parental temperaments will find the leadership aspect easier, and the sanguine and phlegmatic parental temperaments will find the relationship aspect easier. Both, however, must be cultivated.

## Keeping the Ships on Course

Art was giving a talk on temperaments and kids when an older gentleman raised his hand and cautioned the audience: "Don't make the mistake I did when my kids were younger. When they brought home their report cards, I always focused on the one or two B's or C's, and didn't give them credit for their A's. Now they tell me that they never felt I appreciated their hard work." By temperament, he was inclined to be somewhat pessimistic, focusing on what needed to be accomplished and neglecting simple affirmation and words of appreciation. This parent was a strong leader, but he neglected the second ship, relationship.

In parenting, it is vitally important to know our *own* temperament and to be aware of our personal preferences and hot buttons. If I am a melancholic dad, I should be wary lest I react too negatively when my child comes home with a C on a quiz. Instead, I should congratulate him on work well done and, when I am in a receptive and calm mood, sit down with him to discuss how he will improve. If I am a phlegmatic, I will want to make sure I am not avoiding those necessary yet difficult moments of confrontation with my children. If I am a sanguine parent, I may be more inclined to be a buddy to my kids than to parent them, and I might end up forcing my spouse into the "bad guy" role. And if I am a choleric, I will want to watch out that I am not overbearing and pushy to the point of squelching my children's own personality and initiative. These are just a few of the many reasons we need to be sensitive to the chemistry between our temperaments.

So what kind of parent are you? And what is your temperament? Let's try the following short, humorous quiz to identify your parental temperament.

■ ■ ■

*You are homeschooling your elementary school child. It's time for math class. Little Archimedes (Archie, for*

**short) tells you he wants to watch The Price is Right for math.**

a. You say, "No way! Math is at 10:00 a.m. sharp and there's no discussion!"
b. You say, "Great idea! That sounds like a fun way to practice our math skills!"
c. You are in the kitchen, baking pumpkin muffins from scratch.
d. You reply cagily, "I'll let you watch it if you do five math problems in ten minutes first."

**You bring your toddler to Mass; you've brought soft books and quiet toys. What happens next?**

a. You didn't bring toys. Children should pay attention at Mass and follow along with the readings.
b. When Chatty Cathy gets tired of playing with the quiet toys, you encourage her to play with the kids in the pew in front of you. Their toys are way cooler.
c. You let your spouse handle the kids. You are too tired.
d. Soft books and quiet toys are for girly men. You don't own any.

**Your child comes home with a detention for talking in class. The coach threatens to bench him. Your reaction:**

a. He is grounded for six months. You start looking into military schools.
b. You chuckle, "I served detention for three straight weeks when I was your age, son! I'll talk to Coach, and we'll get this straightened out."
c. You let your spouse handle it.
d. You are angry. MJ is the star player! Why, that lousy team wouldn't win a game without him! You know

*of a high school that would love to have him on the team, and it won't hassle him for minor infractions. You put in a call to the dean of students.*

■ ■ ■

In this admittedly exaggerated quiz, (a) is melancholic, (b) sanguine, (c) phlegmatic, and (d) choleric. In this chapter we will explore just how our *own* temperament affects our parenting style. What are the knee-jerk reactions, hot buttons, and pet peeves that are part of our own temperamental bias? We can be sure that our kids will push those buttons and test the limits of our patience. Forewarned is forearmed.

Let's go into a little more detail about each of the four types of parents.[3]

## THE CHOLERIC PARENT

A choleric parent is captain of the ship, leader of the family, divine-right monarch of his own small country. He takes charge with energy, magnanimity, and verve. Everyone in the family will have to keep up or get left behind. He demands loyalty, admiration, and respect. His children are the troops, his spouse the second-in-command, and he leads the charge toward excellence in academics or sports or financial success. His rallying cry is: "He who hesitates is lost!" Or better: "Oo-rah!"

Choleric Frank Gilbreth was a pioneering industrial engineer; his children recorded their family life in the book *Cheaper by the Dozen*. Gilbreth took charge of his twelve kids and ran his home with an eye to efficiency and productivity. When he whistled, they came running, skidding into the parlor in a manner of seconds. The entire family was supposed to "count motions" — whether shaving, showering, or getting dressed — to ensure efficiency in all tasks.

A choleric parent takes his role as head of the household seriously. He is protective, loyal, motivating, and inspiring. So many young minds to mold, so much wisdom to impart. The choleric parent, however, runs the risk of becoming a drill sergeant, creating an atmosphere of command-and-control rather than leadership. One choleric dad says that, when it's time for everyone to leave for school, he warns the kids: "If you're not in the van on time, we're leaving without you." He reports that he has to leave someone only once, and *voilà!* Lesson learned.

This applies to female cholerics as well. One choleric mom we know is the director of a medical clinic, coaches her kids' sports teams, and volunteers at school — all while keeping her large brood in military order. A choleric wife needs to watch out that she doesn't completely dominate, leaving her husband out of the picture.

Choleric parents are strong-willed initiators and sometimes have difficulty relating to small children, especially when these children are quiet, passive, or slow moving. If the activity (like many parenting duties) is boring or seems pointless, such as changing diapers or playing endless rounds of Go Fish, the choleric might delegate the activity and go to the office. A choleric parent may struggle especially to understand a phlegmatic child: "Why isn't he doing more? Why is he so quiet? Is there something *wrong* with that child?" And, if he has a melancholic child, he may wonder why the child seems indecisive or unresponsive.

## *"Because I Said So!"*

If the choleric dad is also partly melancholic, he might tend to severity or harshness or a somewhat judgmental aloofness. He might fall prey to the mistaken notion that too much affection or empathy makes kids soft, weak, or ill prepared. "Because I said so!" is a favorite expression. He will expect his children to simply obey without question, stick to the rules, and get excellent grades with minimal assistance. Cholerics like to pull themselves up by their bootstraps and wonder why anyone else would need warm fuzzies, long explanations, or hands-on assistance to motivate them.

A choleric parent needs to be aware that all children of all temperaments need affection, words of affirmation, gentle encouragement, and time to grow and mature. Two choleric dads we know, both entrepreneurs, told us that they can never relax unless they see a sense of urgency and commitment to action on the part of their employees, their spouse, and their kids. They don't understand why others are not as self-motivated and as self-starting as they are.

It can be a challenge for the choleric to see things from another point of view and to realize that some people of other temperaments do not have an equal sense of urgency or outwardly *convey* their understanding. A choleric (especially if partly melancholic) can be overbearing and dismissive, may overlook the quieter children, and can intimidate everyone through his temper. Some children may actually become fearful of this sort of parent and withdraw or become anxious. One choleric mom who had cowed her family into submission wondered why her offspring were so timid and hesitant. She didn't realize that they were all afraid to open their mouths in her presence! If the choleric parent is partly sanguine, he may be less intimidating, but he will keep his family hopping: whether in sports activities or on grand adventures, his family will be on the go. Just remember that kids need quiet time and relaxing conversations, as well as doubleheaders, to maintain a close relationship with their parents.

Dealing with their children can teach choleric parents patience, humility, and flexibility. One choleric dad who hoped that his oldest son would follow in his footsteps and enter a military academy had to give up that goal when the young man's less-than-stellar GPA made this unattainable. He discovered that his son had many other talents and aspirations, and he adjusted his own sights accordingly. It is important for choleric parents to remember to express unconditional love — our children should know they are loved, even when they aren't little Mini-Me's.

Raising happy and well-adjusted children requires balancing high expectations with affection and warmth. An overly demanding choleric dad who sets high standards but fails to be responsive to his children's needs can alienate his children, possibly even pushing them away from faith and family.[4]

One choleric dad went ballistic when he found out that his smart, serious daughter was dating an unsavory character. He wanted to forbid her ever to see him again. His wise wife cautioned him that doing so could alienate the daughter and drive her into her boyfriend's arms. Instead, they engaged their daughter in an unthreatening discussion, inviting her to tell them why she loved him. In the process of discussing the young man, she herself began to admit certain problems, and eventually the relationship fizzled.

## THE MELANCHOLIC PARENT

The melancholic parent, unlike the sanguine, has *rules*. And he expects compliance with those rules. The melancholic takes his role as parent seriously. His is a noble calling, a divine vocation, and he does not suffer fools gladly. Melancholic parents tend to be demanding of themselves — and their children. One melancholic dad we know had a "perfect" relationship with his firstborn, a melancholic like himself. She achieved perfect grades, was perfectly obedient, and followed house rules perfectly. His next child, however, was not melancholic, and this dad was completely baffled. He didn't know how to relate to a rowdy, bouncy, goof-off sanguine.

Like choleric parents, melancholics will be tempted to control their children, but in less obvious ways. They have rules and expectations, and the consequences for breaking or failing to live up to them include the melancholic parent's tendency to indulge in the brooding glance, the heavy sigh, and the eye-roll to convey displeasure and disappointment. And kids can be very disappointing. They are messy, loud, disobedient, and forgetful, especially if they are sanguine or choleric kids.

Although children may think that they would prefer the sanguine or phlegmatic parent's flexibility and easy distractibility, there are drawbacks. A melancholic parent's sense of order, predictability, and consistent rules will ensure that their children feel safe and secure, as well as reinforce strong morals, personal responsibility, and their Catholic faith. Research has shown that children do well with rules and expectations, and too much flexibility or too many freewheeling options make them insecure, anxious, or "parentified."

Small children thrive with structure and order — they love having special baskets in which to put their toys, helping to cook by following a recipe, and having a set time each day to rest, read, or nap. But clear expectations and rules help teens as well — even though they will not admit this. Teens are faced with an alarming array of confusing options, from alcohol and drugs to unsupervised time after work and school. Clear parental guidelines can give them an "out" and a goal to shoot for. Melancholic parents provide structure in an otherwise capricious world, setting their expectations high with clear and unwavering rules. Dinner is on time, there is a set limit to phone use or playing video games, study time will be blissfully quiet, and the home is beautiful in its serenity and order. This is very comforting to children and teens.

## Be Perfect, Not a Perfectionist

Melancholic parents will insist on telling the truth about Santa, may quote Aquinas when the dog dies, and have no qualms about letting the team suffer if the child is grounded. The child should have thought about the upcoming soccer tournament before she came in late from that date!

They see it as their duty to have rows of perfectly behaved children in the front pew at Mass, children who do their chores and come home on time, and toddlers who answer "to know, love, and serve God" on cue. But what if one of the children is a squirmy, distractible sanguine, a stubborn choleric, or a daydreaming phlegmatic? The melancholic parent, faced with disorder in the ranks, is tempted to deal unduly punitively with the miscreants who dare to act like, well, children.

Melancholic parents place a high value on all that is good, beautiful, and true, and they want to impart this love to their children. They will play classical music in the home, surround themselves with works of art, institute afternoon high tea, and read only the "Great Works" of literature. This is a beautiful and noble way to raise children; however, a melancholic parent can, on occasion, take it too far, and then it backfires. One melancholic mom, in her effort to instill a love for the great works of literature, forbade her children to read any work written after 1962. Unfortunately, this only served to whet her children's appetite for the forbidden fruit, and they became as worldly as the next child — on the sly.

Melancholics should remind themselves that their vocation as parents is not to create the perfect child or to be perfect themselves. Indeed, in this fallen world nothing can be perfect. This is true right down to the mundane details of everyday life. Babies cry, milk spills, dogs bark, and moms don't always have time to clean the house. But it's hard for melancholics to let go of perfection or their view of the way things *ought* to be.

We were alone in the adoration chapel for our scheduled weekly hour, enjoying the serenity of the quiet chapel, the red glow of the tabernacle light, and the candles flickering in the softly lit room. Suddenly, the door swung open to the sound of high heels clicking. The lights sprang into glaring high gear. A melancholic had just entered, and no matter how things had been, now they would be put right — the room lit the way it *ought* to be lit. In the melancholic worldview, there is a certain order to things, and other people should simply adjust.

The perfectionist's demands can drive himself crazy, too — he has the same high standards for himself as he does for others, and this can lead to wakeful nights fretting and worrying. But when Christ said, "You, therefore, must be perfect, as your heavenly Father is perfect" (Matthew 5:48), he did not mean, "Be a perfectionist." The perfection that Christ calls us to is the perfection of *love*. This is an unconditional love, a sacrificial love. But God knows we aren't there yet. When Christ asks Peter three times (John 21:17), "Do you love me?" he was asking whether Peter could love with a divine love. Peter wasn't ready, but Christ loved him still.

## Two Ships Revisited

Melancholics can sometimes allow the rules to eclipse the relationship. This means that sometimes they win the battle but lose the war. For example, one melancholic mom was so focused on having her home run like clockwork that she failed to notice that her oldest child was struggling with depression and anxiety. Another melancholic parent issued an ultimatum to his son: "If you disobey the rules of this house one more time, you are out!" The child disobeyed and left home. Severing the relationship meant that the parents had no further opportunities to teach this child: he was out on the streets. It is very difficult for a melancholic parent to sacrifice his standards in the interest of flexibility, keeping the lines of communication open.

The melancholic parent's high expectations must be accompanied by warmth and affection, with genuine responsiveness to the child's needs. Without this *affective* aspect, parental demands become sheer authoritarianism, which can lead to discouragement or even rebellion. Rules are excellent as long as the child or teen feels that you will listen to him and at least *consider* his perspective or be open and flexible if necessary. To do so is to keep in mind the two ships: leadership and relationship. For example, we've always held to the motto that nothing good happens after midnight, and we tailored curfews accordingly. On one occasion, though, our son wanted to attend a concert of one of his favorite bands. There was no way he could get back before 2:00 a.m., after taking the metro in DC to the outlying parking lot and then driving home. We discussed it and agreed to a later curfew.

## THE SANGUINE PARENT

Kids love a sanguine mom or dad. Since he's a big kid himself, the sanguine typically relates well to his own children and to their friends. He is flexible and entertaining, always ready for a game of hide-and-seek or touch football in the backyard. "The neighborhood kids want to hang at our house? Sure, bring them all over — the more, the merrier! We'll order pizza!"

The sanguine parent is the one who comes up with the creative science project simulating volcanic eruptions or whips up an impromptu Broadway Review starring all of the neighborhood kids. Sanguine parents volunteer abundantly at their children's schools, going beyond ordinary lunch duty or bake-sale donations to driving the activities bus, renovating classrooms, substitute teaching, and coaching. They are restless if they're not involved personally, and they are rarely punitive or repressive. Rules, schmules! Rules are mere guidelines.

But like most temperamental qualities, these inclinations can be a mixed blessing. Sanguine parents can put so much effort into spending quality time with their children and fostering a fun relationship that structure and discipline are forgotten. Sanguine Dad wants to watch Monday Night Football with his boys rather than helping them with homework. If the non-sanguine parent nixes a shopping spree, the kids know where to turn. One stay-at-home sanguine mom, after spending an action-packed day shopping, volunteering at the school, and talking on the phone with friends, met her husband at the door as he returned home from work with a perky "What shall we do for dinner tonight?" His shoulders sagged as he hesitantly replied, "Uh, I thought you were going to handle that!"

Sanguines love their rose-colored glasses. Their sunny temperament always looks on the bright side, and they believe in putting on a happy face. If they have a non-sanguine spouse, he or she may view this optimistic and effervescent attitude as superficiality or problem avoidance. Sometimes sanguines can rightly be accused of sticking their head in the sand or of sheer naïveté. The non-sanguine spouse may begin to feel that he is the only one who takes anything seriously — whether finances, discipline, or marital issues — and may resent doing all the heavy lifting, whether it means disciplining the kids, trying to stick to a budget, setting limits to fun activities, enforcing a curfew, or making sure the homework is done.

When child-raising problems arise (and they always do!), a sanguine parent may be tempted to gloss over them, hoping that his big smile, pat on the back, and optimistic outlook will do the trick. He may prefer minimizing problems, hoping for the best and trusting they will disappear. Even if it's true that ninety percent of all worries never come to pass, the sanguine might miss the early warning signs of serious trouble. It may also be a struggle for a sanguine parent to connect with a quiet, reticent (for example, melancholic) child. Wanting to cure him of "antisocial" behavior, a sanguine may take over and speak for a shy child, forcing him into social situations, usually with counterproductive results. A sanguine parent can overwhelm a more introverted child to the point that the child gives up even trying to get a word in edgewise.

It often happens that a sanguine marries a melancholic (opposites do attract), and the sanguine is tempted to leave all the discipline up to the melancholic, who seems to take naturally to the role as disciplinarian and harbinger of doom. But this is not fair to the melancholic, who then gets branded as the grumpy parent or the "bad cop." It's really much better for parents to participate equally in the disciplining of the kids and for both to participate in the fun times. We are not saying that parents must always present a united front, because we believe that it is healthful and instructive for children to see their parents disagree amiably and work together to find resolutions. However, we do believe that one parent should never be forced to be the sole disciplinarian.

## Reconciling Your Parenting Styles

In *The Temperament God Gave Your Spouse*, we relate the story of sanguine Kyle and melancholic Lydia,[5] who were struggling to reconcile their opposite parenting styles, which were based on their very opposite temperaments. Though they shared core values and their Catholic faith, they had radically different approaches to parenting, and this was a source of conflict between them. Kyle wanted to be flexible and open to his kids' socializing and extracurricular activities, while Lydia tended to worry about the details, checking the interim grades, frequently contacting teachers, monitoring the teens' cell-phone calls and computer time, and fretting about their messy rooms. As we point out in the book, Kyle and Lydia were caught in a classic tug-of-war between opposite temperaments: the sanguine feeling that he had to be *more* tolerant and optimistic because the melancholic was overly critical, while the melancholic felt that she had to crack down even harder because the sanguine wasn't taking their kids' problems seriously!

Just recognizing that parenting styles are often temperament-based helps relieve the stress and arguments. The key is to sit down and discuss your parenting goals as a team: for example, we want our kids to do well in school, but we realize that there is a learning curve, so we will allow a little time for adjustment before we start cracking down; or we both want the kids to dress nicely for Mass, so let's go to Saturday evening Mass if we would otherwise have to run straight to church from Sunday soccer practice.

Once both parents recognize that they have the same goal — raising kids who do their best in school and have respect for the faith — they can work out the details of how to achieve these ends.

## THE PHLEGMATIC PARENT

Phlegmatic parents are patient, easygoing, and value a peaceful home. They are often found enjoying the simple things of life: playing catch in the backyard, taking their kids fishing, reading favorite bedtime stories over and over, and fixing up a batch of homemade cookies. They are soothing and comfortable, like an old shoe. A phlegmatic mom is thrifty, gentle, and loves staying home with the kids. A phlegmatic dad is Christ-like in service to his family, solid and hardworking, a man of few words. Phlegmatics set a positive example of moderation, dependability, and simplicity.

But there were times when Christ turned the other cheek and a time when he turned over the tables. The phlegmatic's default setting is to appease, to compromise, to wait and see. But sometimes ignoring a problem doesn't work, especially when it comes to raising kids. A child who can't seem to catch on to reading, the youngster with no friends, the teen whose grades are steadily slipping — these are issues that must be addressed. It can be a cross for the peaceful phlegmatic to turn off the TV, discipline the angry teen, take an unpopular stand, say no to the boss, make the final decisions, and tackle problems head-on.

Because the phlegmatic has a hard time being demanding, insistent, or even intrusive, he may leave discipline to the more assertive spouse. He may wait for problems to occur rather than take a pro-active stance on academics and other concerns. We have a friend who is an easygoing, soft-spoken phlegmatic engineer. He meticulously maintains his yard, raking leaves, trimming bushes, and keeping up a lawn that rivals a golf-course putting green. We were surprised when his teenage son and his friends starting playing baseball in the backyard, tearing up the grass, smashing the ball into the fence, and knocking down fence posts and even the swing set. Then we realized that because of our friend's phlegmatic nature, he didn't want to interrupt his son's eager enjoyment of the outdoors.

Instead of raising a fuss, he himself took down the demolished swing set, replanted grass seed, replaced the fence boards, and installed a large net. Because he didn't want to make a fuss, however, he missed the opportunity to teach his kids some valuable handyman skills and the importance of cleaning up their messes. Though they learned the lesson that their dad is totally supportive of their athletic growth, they may have also learned that someone else will clean up after them. Sometimes kids need a little in-your-face-style confrontation that the easygoing phlegmatic finds hard to deliver.

Still, children will generally benefit from the stability that a phlegmatic parent provides. The phlegmatic's even temper, patience, and capacity for withstanding abuse also make him ideally suited to raising teenagers! Because phlegmatics are so easygoing and patient, and have such an accepting and comforting way of dealing with children, it is rare for such parents to incite in their offspring intense rebellion or anger — especially if the kids have inherited the same temperament from Mom or Dad. But even when they have different temperaments, the children of phlegmatic parents tend to go about their business of work and school without causing any major trouble.

That doesn't mean that parenting is always a breeze for phlegmatic parents. These conflict-avoiding folks may find themselves taken aback or nonplussed by an extremely outgoing, demanding, or argumentative child, and they could mistake some of those different attitudes for rebellion. In such cases, it helps for these parents to understand that other temperaments exhibit different behaviors and to be reassured by trusted friends and teachers that their children are behaving within an acceptable norm for kids their age. On the other hand, if phlegmatic parents don't go out of their way — it won't come naturally to them — to provide their kids with a strong family structure that encourages effort and excellence, they might settle for less than their kids are capable of. This is especially true for their phlegmatic children.

But even a quiet, easygoing phlegmatic can become upset, especially if he's been stuffing his feelings for a long time. Phlegmatic Ben[6] had been tolerant of his wife Annie's nagging for many months: the honey-do list, the neglected yard work, her concerns about the grades of one of her kids, and (on the meta-level) her worries about his lack of communication. He had patiently put up with stress at work combined with her nagging without ever acknowledging the toll this was taking on him. One day the simmering pot hit boil, and he burst out in anger, shocking himself and Annie. A conflict-avoidant phlegmatic can endure suppressed anger for a long time, but even he may explode in rage — or worse, walk away tight-lipped.

Ben eventually learned to address his problems as they happened, instead of continually putting his feelings on the back burner. He finally shared his worries about work and his frustration about being nagged. Ben and Annie agreed to work together to help their children with homework so that the burden of discipline would not fall entirely on one person's shoulders. Ben began demanding more from his kids in terms of the household chores. These changes require courage and initiative for a non-confrontational phlegmatic.

When the quiet and easygoing phlegmatic parent steps up to the plate as spiritual head of the family, he becomes a particularly strong leader: one who leads naturally through humble service and quiet generosity.

\*\*\*

Each of the four temperaments has its own natural strengths — whether it's the take-charge enthusiasm of the choleric, the high ideals of the melancholic, the friendly optimism of the sanguine, or the soothing peacefulness of the phlegmatic.

Yet parenting calls us to reach higher and to step outside our comfort zone — especially when we have a new baby, a sick child, a tough school situation, or other difficulties that cause stress for the family. We need strength from prayer and the sacraments. We need to stretch ourselves beyond our own temperament in order to engage our children effectively: the choleric parent slows down and listens empathically, the melancholic relaxes, the sanguine holds firm, and the phlegmatic takes charge.

■ ■ ■

### Choleric Parent at a Glance

- *Strong leadership of the family.*
- *Protective, demands loyalty.*
- *Can be overbearing, dismissive, and lack empathy.*
- *May overlook or overpower quiet, retiring children.*
- *Leans into tough issues.*
- *Leads with "Let's do it!"*

### Melancholic Parent at a Glance

- *Serious.*
- *Values truth, beauty, self-sacrifice, rules, high ideals.*
- *Relationship and motivational skills are less developed.*
- *May be perfectionistic, critical, worried, inflexible, micromanaging.*

- *Leans into tough issues.*
- *Leads with "No!"*

## Sanguine Parent at a Glance

- *Fun-loving, relationship-oriented.*
- *Flexible, adventurous, playful, involved.*
- *Motivates with enthusiasm.*
- *May be inconsistent with discipline, order, rules, and structure.*
- *May avoid tough issues.*
- *Leads with "Why not? Sounds fun!"*

## Phlegmatic Parent at a Glance

- *Quiet, easygoing, accepting, empathic, non-demanding.*
- *Values harmony, peace, cooperation.*
- *May withdraw, appear indifferent, or fail to take on leadership role.*
- *May avoid tough issues.*
- *Leads with "I understand."*

■ ■ ■

# CHAPTER 7

# PARENT-CHILD
# TEMPERAMENTAL INTERACTION

*A goodness of fit between parent and child does not necessarily
involve similarity of temperament between the two.*
STELLA CHESS AND ALEXANDER THOMAS

Parenting is an awesome responsibility and a wonderful,
exhilarating, and occasionally frustrating endeavor. And
although the focus of parenting is, of course, on children, we
parents have to take the first step in understanding ourselves
so that we can begin to understand our children. The wisdom
we gain will enable us to lead our family, helping our children
fulfill the promise and mission God has given each of them.

As we consider our temperament in relation to the temperaments of our children, we see where we are similar and
different, how we can avoid unnecessary power struggles, and
how we might adapt our parenting style to suit the needs of
each child.

■ ■ ■

### How Do Kids of Different Temperaments
### Seek Parental Attention?

- **Melancholics** might whine, cry, complain, argue a fine
  point, or have a meltdown.

- **Cholerics** may do something special or exceptional and want to receive credit. They might demand, be angry, or argue.
- **Sanguines** love to be the center of attention. They might laugh, tell a funny story, be silly, or interrupt.
- **Phlegmatics** will hang around or simply hope that you will notice them.

■■■

# THE CHOLERIC PARENT

## Choleric Parent/Choleric Child

Cholerics want to have an opinion on everything and simply cannot resist a good debate. How many arguments between Laraine and Lucy have been sparked by this match-and-flint relationship? Neither can leave a debatable subject untouched: each must pounce on the topic like a dog with a chew toy and counter the proposition or insist on a different view! But these sparring matches are usually friendly, and neither Laraine nor Lucy harbors long-lasting resentment.

The wise choleric parent will learn to identify sacrosanct rules and key issues from which he will not budge, and let the minor points go. He should learn to pick his battles, or the home life will become an unbearable war zone. At some point, the bell has to ring and the fight must come to an end, even if not completely resolved. This is the parent's responsibility. Once the choleric child realizes that his parent is not going to back down on key issues, he will (eventually) learn to submit his strong will. The independence of the choleric is an advantage in that the child wants to handle for himself many tasks for which more timid children insist on parental assistance.

For his part, the choleric parent is fairly hands-off and less likely to be buzzing around nervously like a helicopter parent. A choleric parent might be *too* willing to allow independence in his choleric child and thereby miss opportunities for instruction and example that would teach virtues and morals. Nonetheless, a choleric parent will appreciate his offspring's competitive nature, his industriousness, and his strong will. The key will be channeling that will and drive toward the good and balancing his competitive spirit with compassion.

## Choleric Parent/Melancholic Child

A choleric parent might be baffled by a quiet, reflective, melancholic child who doesn't readily jump into new activities, make friends quickly, or easily join conversations. Be careful lest you speak for your child or push him to do things for which he isn't ready. Don't expect high energy, mature sociability, and full-blown initiative in the melancholic child when he is quite small. One choleric we know expressed puzzlement over those children on his sports team who weren't motivated by sheer competition but instead needed lots of reassurance, words of encouragement, team-building activities, and other motivations to perform. In the choleric's view, everyone should be self-starting and already motivated.

A choleric parent may become irritated by his melancholic's complaining or detail gathering or persistence. He will want to shout, "Let's get moving!" But strong leadership requires an equally strong relationship: take the time to really *listen* to your melancholic. Support and encourage him, and then lead him.

The melancholic is particularly sensitive and may not exhibit outward indications of responsiveness. Furthermore, some children take a while to blossom, and pushing them will not help this process along — in fact, it is likely to drive the melancholic deeper into his shell. Though you don't want to take over for him and solve all his problems, you do want to gently encourage him to find his own solutions. In fact, the two of you can find common ground in seeking the *quality* solution: the choleric wants to solve the problem, and the melancholic wants to do it well.

A melancholic child gives the assertive choleric parent an opportunity to become a more sensitive and patient parent, one more open to the "soft" skills of communication — listening and empathy. Once the choleric parent realizes that the melancholic child needs to mature at his own speed, he can be very helpful in the process. A choleric parent can guide and model initiative, standing up for oneself, and sociability.

### Choleric Parent/Sanguine Child

A choleric parent might mistakenly assume that his happy-go-lucky, talkative sanguine is perfectly capable of growing up on his own without significant parental intervention. The choleric would like to think so because he finds some of the more mundane parenting tasks quite tedious. He thinks: "Why can't the child just handle this himself? I did!" But the affectionate and distractible sanguine child is not like the independent, driven choleric. This child needs his parents to set limits, give clear guidance, and provide structure.

A sanguine often asks for — and usually demands — attention. He keeps up a nonstop stream of talk, interspersed with requests: to play a game with you, to go shopping with you, to invite friends over, to go to the park, and on and on. Sometimes the choleric parent wants to say, "Stop fooling around!" But it's important occasionally to allow for some fun times with no agenda, just you and your happy child.

After strengthening your relationship (playing catch, going to the movies, or chatting over a cup of coffee, for example) you can take the opportunity to impart some key skills. Through your leadership, you can teach your scattered sanguine how to organize his projects, break big tasks into smaller ones, stay on task, set goals, and plan for the future. And then take some time out to enjoy your delightful sanguine child. You will not regret it.

## Choleric Parent/Phlegmatic Child

One high-powered, successful choleric parent of a low-key phlegmatic expressed his puzzlement: "I don't understand this kid at all! What motivates him?" He thought his child was passive, unambitious, and even lazy. He doubted that his son would be able to survive in the tough business world in which the dad thrived. He told this to his son, thinking his displeasure would motivate him to change. In fact, his son was neither lazy nor unmotivated — just very, very different from his dad. Instead of serving to motivate him, his dad's negative attitude and constant criticism caused the boy to withdraw, fearing that he would disappoint his father further. He was so discouraged that he began hiding in his room, playing video games and in general behaving in an even *less* motivated fashion!

When the dad sought family counseling, Art challenged him to help his son *succeed*. The methods that would have motivated the father — expressing disappointment, challenging him to be aggressive — would not motivate his son. Art asked the dad to recall his son's athletic accomplishments and reminded him that the boy couldn't have been such a good athlete without the virtues of perseverance and fortitude. He suggested that the father immediately stop nagging and criticizing, work on the relationship first, and begin to praise his son enthusiastically for his successes in school and in sports. The boy soon began to perk up.

In fact, the choleric parent's passion and enthusiasm can be infectious and help motivate his child to discover his own strengths and pursue his goals. With structure and support, phlegmatics can be very competitive in sports, academics, and business. With their humble, hardworking ethic, they can achieve significant goals — but they do need overt praise and encouragement as well as direction when setting goals and identifying milestones. A critical approach will not fly.

Aggressive challenges and dares will also fail to motivate the phlegmatic. Lead with praise and support, and help him to discover and pursue his dreams: "Remember when you used to get up every morning at 4:00 a.m. to skate? You have great perseverance and fortitude! I know you can handle this new job!"

Choleric parents can help their phlegmatic children learn to stand up for themselves and to step outside their comfort zone when necessary. They should understand, however, that their easygoing children will have their own quiet way of doing these things, and that way will be unlike the approach of their more vocal parents. Sometimes this quiet self-assurance can be even more effective than the noisier self-assurance of the choleric.

# The Melancholic Parent

## Melancholic Parent/Choleric Child

The challenge for a deeply introspective, idealistic, melancholic parent? To resist the temptation to engage the choleric in power struggles that will provoke him to rebellion. You are both committed and unwavering in your views, though you may not express yourself quite as vocally as the choleric. Further, you, the parent, tend to be more sensitive than your choleric child, and you feel deeply hurt when he openly disagrees with you. You believe in your heart that he should not argue with you — ever. Nor should he disagree, even internally. Children should do what they are told, follow the rules, and never talk back.

A choleric child seems mouthy, oppositional, and even belligerent. A melancholic might be tempted to punish such a child for argumentativeness or overly energetic behavior. It is important to reflect on the child's behavior and your own reaction, and to distinguish between behavior that is clearly wrong and disrespectful and behavior that is simply annoying or persistent. A melancholic parent might *feel* as though he is being disrespected when in fact the choleric is only voicing an alternate opinion. It is often more instructive to allow for a give-and-take of ideas and feelings than to clamp down in a repressive and controlling way.

And if you find yourself being too harsh, apologize and promise to be more empathic next time. Try to focus more on the relationship, and a little less on maintaining control. Keep in mind that melancholic parents (more than parents of other temperaments) tend to draw a line in the sand when more subtle forms of negotiation would be preferable. Showing mercy and giving a second chance don't necessarily convey weakness.

Sometimes it is hard for melancholics to express overt appreciation, especially when they don't think it's necessary or deserving. However, all children, but especially cholerics, need to hear that their gifts and talents are appreciated within the family.

## Melancholic Parent/Melancholic Child

Ah, the blessings of a quiet house, where each respects the other's space, solitude, and rules. You understand each other and relate well on principles and order. You both will happily spend an evening reading and listening to Mahler. A perfectionist, melancholic child will be the apple of her melancholic parent's eye. But watch out lest the two of you become overly caught up in a hyper-vigilant perfectionism that creates anxiety in the entire family. Ask yourself, as the parent in this scenario: Do people breathe a sigh of relief when you are not home? Do they walk on eggshells when you are? If so, you might be creating an aura of tension and stress because of your critical and perfectionist demands, and you will be encouraging the same tendencies in your melancholic child.

Even though you have only the best of intentions, sometimes you will need to take a much-needed break and settle for less. Encourage your melancholic child to develop friendships, a social life, and charitable works that take her beyond the usual academic environment. Both of you are likely to be artistic or musical, and together you can enjoy artistic expression in dramatic arts, music, and other creative outlets.

One melancholic parent we know had always had high expectations and had been very strict about the rules. His kids were expected to do chores on time, excel in school, and never squirm at Mass. Unfortunately, one of the kids was a quiet perfectionist who struggled with depression, but his parents never discovered this until it was almost too late and the child had to be hospitalized. What was needed was a little more one-on-one time, relaxed conversations after dinner, some fun activities together, dinners out, and so forth. These would have helped create an atmosphere in which the child could feel comfortable revealing his deepest fears and anxieties. Sanguine and choleric kids will have no trouble making themselves and their needs known, but the introverted melancholic may not do so.

## Melancholic Parent/Sanguine Child

The melancholic parent is serious, reflective, and values a quiet and tidy home atmosphere. The sanguine child, on the other hand, is likely to be noisy, energetic, distractible, and scattered. These temperamental opposites are ripe for conflict, especially if the melancholic parent thinks the sanguine child is behaving this way to willfully defiant.

For example, you tell your sanguine child to come home promptly after playing with his neighbor because he has a music lesson. The child, however, is distracted by a game of basketball with his friends and completely forgets about the lesson. He arrives home late to parental wrath. Or the sanguine child routinely forgets to study for tests until they're practically upon him. The melancholic parent, even as a child, would never have forgotten the lesson or the tests and so finds himself completely bemused. He may believe the child is being disobedient on purpose and in need of punishment. But if the melancholic parent patiently continues to provide clear rules and set firm limits, he is the most capable of helping a sanguine child get organized and stay focused.

A wise parent will take additional measures when dealing with the effervescent sanguine: send text reminders on his cell phone, leave a message with the friend's parents, write his class schedule on his arm…. A melancholic parent might be tempted to think, "He simply ought to remember! I shouldn't have to jump through hoops!" But though this would work for a conscientious melancholic or a dutiful phlegmatic, it's an unrealistic approach for a sanguine and doomed to result in many more lectures, punishments, and groundings than would otherwise be necessary. It is critically important to realize that he is just not like you! Many of these behaviors that you find frustrating are temperamental traits rather than examples of wrongdoing.

Try not to squelch the sanguine's eager enthusiasm and fun-loving attitude through too much criticism or inflexibility. Stay connected, and enjoy this lively and enthusiastic child. Your natural instinct for structure, organization, and rules will be a boon to the sanguine, who struggles with self-control and with setting his own limits.

## Melancholic Parent/Phlegmatic Child

A dual melancholic couple told us about their aimless twenty-something phlegmatic child: they were letting him stay in their home for six months, and then it was time to get out — whether or not he had found a job! Tough love, baby!

A melancholic parent is likely to be tempted to micromanage a phlegmatic child. And the phlegmatic will let him do so, but it is often not in the child's best interest. The phlegmatic child will someday need to defend himself on the playground, speak up in class, and decide on a college major. Sit down with him to discuss his dreams and goals, encourage him to speak up, and use role-playing to help him gain confidence.

A phlegmatic child often struggles most with discouragement. His sweet disposition and cooperative spirit lead him to downplay his own needs and to acquiesce to other, stronger wills. Sometimes this leads to sub-par performance. A melancholic parent is not always attuned to the importance of motivating and enthusiastically supporting his kids: he believes that everyone ought to do what they are supposed to do, and not require extra attention or hand-holding. But this may be just what your low-key phlegmatic needs in order to get moving. Try not to nag, scold, or lecture, which tends to discourage phlegmatics even more because they take things very personally.

## The Sanguine Parent

### Sanguine Parent/Choleric Child

Sanguine parents typically are hearty, fun-loving, and relationship-oriented. Such parents can handle choleric children, provided they can stay firm when necessary and refuse to let the choleric's argumentative ways get under their skin. In other words, the sanguine parent should try not to be wounded or offended when the choleric launches into a debate. A choleric child will want reasons and explanations, while a sanguine parent might deal more in hunches or impressions. Nonetheless, it's important to stay calm and rational, especially in the middle of a choleric argument.

The sanguine parent can help the choleric develop compassion, sensitivity, and empathy, gentle virtues that are vital to the choleric. Spending one-on-one time together can provide great opportunities to transmit these virtues and values, and the typically independent choleric will enjoy such time together, especially if you let him choose the activity.

The greatest danger with this parent-child temperament combination is that the easygoing parent might feel intimidated by a particularly strong-willed and demanding choleric child. If the parent continually gives in to the child's demands, he runs the risk of creating a "child tyrant"[1] and a helpless-parent situation. This does not mean that the sanguine parent has to be completely controlling and unresponsive to the child's point of view. He does, however, have to maintain his own expectations and insist that the child obey the rules of the home and treat parents and siblings with respect. For example, if, at the grocery store, a choleric child asks for a treat and begins to wail when refused, a sanguine parent is more likely to appease the child by giving in. This only reinforces the child's belief that all he needs to do is raise a fuss to get what he wants. In a situation like this, the parent can remain responsive to the child while reinforcing rules: "You can't have a treat until after lunch. When you act like that, though, you cannot have a treat at all."

## Sanguine Parent/Melancholic Child

The sanguine parent may find himself as baffled by his melancholic child as the melancholic parent by the sanguine child. One sanguine parent of a melancholic worried that her young child was antisocial because she rarely gave eye contact, hung around the outskirts while the other children were playing, and never spoke when meeting new people. We reassured this parent that her child was completely normal for her temperament and, given time and encouragement, would eventually come out of her shell.

If you are a sanguine, watch out that you aren't doing all of the talking all of the time, teasing too much, or telling funny and embarrassing stories about your melancholic child. Now that her kids are young adults, my sanguine friend Beth finds that they often correct her. Don't exaggerate, they tell her. Don't start dancing at the school dance when you are supposed to be a chaperone. And please don't tell embarrassing college drinking stories!

A melancholic child is not like you, so don't rush him into activities and friendships — and give him plenty of space and time in which to reflect and to share his thoughts with you. Allow quiet time for creative projects, protect him from bullies, and don't push him into activities or friendships if he isn't ready. Don't take his moodiness personally: when your melancholic vents all his frustrations in a negative rant, allow him to work through these issues at his own speed. Lend a sympathetic ear; model confidence and optimism.

When your melancholic is particularly anxious or fretful, you can ask him: "What is the worst that could happen? Is that so bad?" and help him role-play to find solutions. Though you may at times be frustrated by your melancholic's more pessimistic view on life, a sanguine parent needs to learn to slow down, stop talking, and really *listen* to his melancholic child. Even though these children are not overtly expressive of their appreciation, know that your melancholic values your support. Your enthusiasm is infectious. Encourage and support your melancholic, and help him initiate new projects, make new friends, and discover the world.

## Sanguine Parent/Sanguine Child

A sanguine parent paired with a sanguine child can be dynamic and sometimes explosive. Where two or more sanguines are gathered, you have a party. They can egg each other on, compete for attention, tell louder and more exaggerated stories, and overrun the budget. When we were homeschooling, sanguine Sam could sometimes persuade his partly sanguine mother that it would be "educational" to take a trip to the zoo for science class, or pursue any number of other fun activities. At the end of the week, Laraine would wonder why they hadn't covered all their lessons.

The challenge for a sanguine parent will be to provide structure and to set limits. Studies have shown that children who struggle with self-control (as sanguines typically do) need their parents' help in setting limits or they may suffer anxiety and depression. Sanguines need clear structure and firm limits, assistance in breaking big projects into manageable portions, in motivating to persevere, and in learning the importance of hard work in achieving goals.

Sanguine parents are likely to volunteer at their kids' school, know who their children's friends are, and be involved in their activities. This is a great way to stay connected and keep tabs on your kids as well. Focus on the leadership of your family, as well as the relationship aspect, and encourage perseverance and formation in the faith so that both you and your sanguine will build your lives on the firm foundation of Christ, rather than the shifting sands of the world.

## Sanguine Parent/Phlegmatic Child

Our sanguine friend was touring her alma mater with her phlegmatic son and his best friend, who were considering attending the university. At every spot on the campus tour, she would relate a funny or memorable incident. "Oh, I remember the time we drove the car right up the curb, onto the grass, and through the bushes to get to our dorm!" It wasn't long before her phlegmatic son was dying of embarrassment and shooting her quelling glances.

Sanguine parents — encouraging, vocal, motivating — are a boon for a phlegmatic child. They help the child become more expressive of feelings and ideas. Sometimes, as in the example above, the phlegmatic might find himself a little overwhelmed or embarrassed by the sanguine parent's over-the-top storytelling, exaggeration, or involvement. Nonetheless, overt appreciation, adventuresome spirit, and hands-on involvement are just what he needs to grow more lively, interested, and motivated himself. Unless he is encouraged by his parents and friends, a phlegmatic is in danger of becoming withdrawn and mired in complacency. A sanguine may be tempted to nag or tease in an attempt to rouse the phlegmatic into action. Be patient and continue to encourage him. A sanguine parent will be the ideal mentor to keep the phlegmatic child motivated and engaged with the world and others.

■ ■ ■

### Responses to Discipline

- **Cholerics:** *They will refuse to admit they are wrong; they will rage or argue, counterattack.*

- **Melancholics:** *They sulk, feel deeply hurt, and find it hard to forgive.*
- **Sanguines:** *They laugh or charm their way out of it; they become hurt but will forget quickly.*
- **Phlegmatics:** *They accept discipline quietly, dutifully, with resignation.*

■ ■ ■

# THE PHLEGMATIC PARENT

## *Phlegmatic Parent/Choleric Child*

The easygoing and peaceful phlegmatic parent may find himself exhausted by his energetic, outspoken, stubborn choleric. You and your choleric child are complete opposites: you are easygoing, cooperative, and favor compromise rather than debate. He is intense, willful, and relishes conflict. You might think this is a recipe for disaster, but psychologists who study temperament have found this is not necessarily so. Psychiatrists Stella Chess and Alexander Thomas relate a story of a low-key phlegmatic parent who had an extremely intense and often difficult child. Though the two were quite opposite in their emotional responses, this parent appreciated his son's temperament, treated his outbursts with patience and acceptance, and at times even admired how distinct he was from his parents.[2]

But this combination of temperaments can also give rise to conflict. The sensitive and reserved phlegmatic can find the choleric child's argumentativeness and constant engagement exhausting. If you feel as though your authority is being disrespected, you may experience a low-simmering anger or resentment deep inside.

## Leadership and Relationship

| Parent: | Leadership: | Relationship: |
| --- | --- | --- |
| **Choleric child** | Give him reasons for what you ask. Don't fear his strong will. Insist on respectful interaction. Direct him toward truly good and supernatural motives. | Continue to give him love and affection, even when he is argumentative and seemingly independent. Model empathy, compassion, and forgiveness. |
| **Melancholic child** | Help her grow interpersonally and in confidence. Mentor her in life changes. "Kick-start" new projects and social interaction. | Give her words of affirmation (five positive to every one critical comment), frequent positive process comments, and other affirmations (touches, smiles, and so forth). |
| **Sanguine child** | Provide clear rules, expectations, structure, and guidance. Teach him that fun and friends are important, but that he will ultimately achieve true happiness and joy if he also works hard and prays. | Give him credit for his friendliness, enthusiasm, and initiative. Do fun things together: "Let's do something fun. You pick the movie, and I know we'll have a great time!" |
| **Phlegmatic child** | You may have to push her to take chances, to take on leadership, to speak up when it's uncomfortable, to talk about her hopes and dreams. Build confidence by connecting the dots of her previous successes with new ventures. | You need to ask a lot of questions, even when she doesn't initiate discussions. Encourage her with positive support to discover her passion. Help her fight discouragement by reminding her of her strengths and achievements. |

Your patience and tolerance will be a beneficial model for guiding the choleric child to greater compassion, empathy, and patience. Don't let the choleric do whatever he wants or walk all over you. If you do, your child will become a little dictator, and for your part, you will feel — and be — ineffective. Use your diplomatic skills to help him see his own faults and to admit when he is wrong. When a choleric thinks he came up with the insight himself, he will be much more likely to change.

## Phlegmatic Parent/Melancholic Child

One phlegmatic parent of a melancholic child discovered to her chagrin that when the child reached adolescence, he became a sarcastic, grumpy loner who spent hours reading and playing video games. His "friends" were gamers, known only by their virtual-reality names. She realized that she had, perhaps, allowed her introverted child a little too much leeway in choosing the solitary activities he preferred, such as reading and playing video games, and that she had never encouraged him to try other activities. Because of her phlegmatic temperament, she rarely had playgroups at her house or participated in mom-and-tot groups. She'd never signed him up for sports lessons, the scouts, or music lessons.

Here's where the phlegmatic parent will need to be a leader and step outside his comfort zone and initiate those activities that he knows are beneficial for his melancholic child — whether sports, church groups, dance lessons, or school clubs. You will not only need to model interpersonal skills and appropriately assertive behavior, but you will also need to initiate fun social interactions and help your child take advantage of leadership opportunities. Share your thoughts and feelings with your melancholic child. Tell him how you once were very shy but overcame it, or tell him about the valuable lessons you learned as a young kid playing baseball. Never hesitate to praise him overtly.

## Phlegmatic Parent/Sanguine Child

The easygoing, quiet, hard-working phlegmatic parent may find himself baffled by this high-energy, emotionally expressive, and talkative child. He may wonder whether he is doing something wrong since this child seems so intent on trying everything, experimenting, testing limits, and is so distractible. You are not doing anything wrong: this is the sanguine temperament. In fact, your easygoing, good-natured style of parenting is likely to be just the gentle touch the sanguine needs. The sanguine wants to feel connected with you and appreciated by you.

You should, however, watch out that your sanguine doesn't take advantage of your easygoing nature and end up breaking rules (always with a convincing excuse) and getting into trouble (always remorseful afterward). You don't want to disturb that great relationship, and so you might be tempted to give in. Nonetheless, the sanguine needs firm guidance and structure in order to thrive. Don't give up, saying: "He's too distracted!" Use your relationship skills to cultivate strong leadership over this effervescent child. He needs to grow in discipline, perseverance, and self-mastery. You may have to step outside your own laid-back temperament in order to provide the consistent rules and clear limits that this child needs. Here, your firm but positive leadership will be immensely rewarding.

## Phlegmatic Parent/Phlegmatic Child

A match made in heaven! The easygoing and patient parent will appreciate his easygoing and cooperative child. Imagine father and son spending hours quietly fishing together or watching Monday Night Football. Imagine mom and daughter baking bread or playing Candy Land. This is a comfortable, low-key combination, contributing to a peaceful home life. If your other children include an intense choleric, a moody melancholic, or a whirlwind sanguine, you will surely breathe a sigh of relief! Both parent and child will react quietly and respectfully, with the phlegmatic child rarely causing any trouble.

In this scenario, however, a phlegmatic parent may fail to model enthusiasm and passion, and might not provide leadership for the phlegmatic child or teach him how to be an effective leader. This could result in a pattern of underachievement — for both the parent and the child. You will serve this child best by encouraging and modeling virtuous self-assertion and standing up for what is true and good.

***

In order to lead our children well and to cultivate our relationship with each of them, we need to evaluate our temperamental tendencies and be willing to step outside of them in ways that might not feel naturally comfortable. If we do this, we will help our children grow and flourish. This is taking up our cross daily, as our Lord enjoined us. A choleric parent will need to listen with compassion. A melancholic may need to become a cheerleader. A sanguine parent will need to listen and to provide discipline, and a phlegmatic will need to take on leadership. By working to transform our own temperamental weaknesses into strengths, we model self-sacrifice, self-control, and self-giving. And as we teach our children to become mature, loving Christians, we too are sanctified.

# CHAPTER 8

# GROWING IN VIRTUE

*The home is well suited for education in the virtues.*
CATECHISM OF THE CATHOLIC CHURCH (N. 2223)

Every parent wants his children to be happy — not only in this life but also in the next. To this end, we raise them well: we educate them, teach them manners and morals, and help them value the truth and the good. We try to instill in them a love of God and his Church, as well as a love for neighbor. We teach them to pray and to seek their vocation as children of God (CCC 2226). All of this is a huge task, and we are often reminded of how much we truly rely on God's grace.

Parents are the primary educators of their children; we have the first and ultimate responsibility (CCC 2223) to shape our children morally, spiritually, and humanly. The buck stops here. We may send our children to school or teach them at home, according to our decision about what is best for them. We may send them to religious education at our parish or to Catholic school. Our hope is that each one of our children will, like the child Jesus, grow in grace and wisdom.

The Pontifical Council for the Family teaches that each child should receive individualized formation.[1] Our children are unique, each with a unique personality, temperament, and mission from God. One very practical way we can tailor our parenting so that we provide this individualized formation is to take into account their different temperaments, as we discussed in the previous chapter. Most significant, as we teach them to grow in virtue, we need to know what sort of pitfalls they might face, given their temperament.

Our kids' temperaments are a gift from God and part of their nature at birth. Each child's temperament, which cannot be exchanged for another temperament,[2] brings with it certain strengths and weaknesses. Some virtues will be easier or harder to attain. Yet, as Father Conrad Hock wisely advised, "All of man's inclinations and peculiarities should be used for the service of the Lord."[3] It is a parent's job to nurture the strengths, correct the weaknesses, redirect the bad inclinations, and encourage the natural virtues that are nascent in each child's temperament.

Keep in mind that grace never destroys nature but rather builds upon it and perfects it. For example, a choleric is likely to be naturally courageous, while obedience may be challenging. By contrast, the phlegmatic child's naturally docile nature makes compliance and cooperation quite easy, but confrontation is difficult. While the sanguine struggles with perseverance, he exudes natural confidence and joy. A melancholic, by contrast, may find it difficult to express easy confidence, but he will manifest self-control and discipline.

Human nature, created by God in his image, is essentially good. Yet as long as creation is in a state of journeying toward perfection (CCC 310), our temperaments are limited in the same way that all of nature is limited. Furthermore, our nature is wounded through original sin.

Because our nature is not sinful, however, those tendencies that derive from our temperament are not in themselves *culpable*; the weaknesses of our temperaments are not themselves sins. But they can make certain virtues more difficult to acquire, and they can lead us more easily into certain types of sin. For example, melancholics may be more prone to sadness and find it difficult to attain the virtue of supernatural confidence and joy; sanguines tend to be immoderate and impulsive, and attaining the virtues of self-control and perseverance is a true battle. Cholerics struggle with pride and find it difficult to be humble and to express empathy toward others, while phlegmatics may fall into discouragement and need to be encouraged toward holy boldness.

By the same token, though, there are natural virtues that each of the temperaments may find more easily acquired. Though virtue is not the same as personality, there are some correlations between virtue and temperament.[4] For example, melancholics are naturally more disciplined, careful, and rule abiding. Sanguines are, by nature, friendly, empathic, and considerate. Cholerics are resourceful, independent, and purposeful. And phlegmatics are peaceful, patient, and humble.[5] In short, the different temperaments will have a natural predisposition to certain virtues. God gives us just what we need.

In the sections that follow, we will take a look at each of the temperaments and the virtues that might tend to come more easily with each. We will also explore some of the characteristic weakness and temptations of each temperament and ways we parents can *encourage* our children's growth in virtue.

## Cholerics and Virtue

It is said that cholerics make great saints ... or great sinners.[6] Cholerics are motivated self-starters, with abundant zeal and confidence. They are resourceful, purposeful, and focused when pursuing their goals. The key is focusing them on the *right* goal. Cholerics can be just as zealous and focused when pursuing their *own* will instead of God's.

Consider choleric St. Paul. Prior to his conversion, Saul was rabidly anti-Christian and "laid waste" to the Church: barging into homes, dragging off the fledgling Christians, and throwing them in prison (Acts 8:3). But after his encounter with Christ, he became even more fervent in spreading the Gospel. Following his conversion, Scripture tells us that "Saul increased all the more in strength, and confounded the Jews who lived in Damascus by proving that Jesus was the Christ" (Acts 9:22).

He loved to argue and debate, and he didn't care who disagreed with him — even St. Peter, the first pope, was not immune! "I opposed him to his face, because he stood condemned" (Galatians 2:11), Paul writes. In Acts we read about how Paul had been so angry about John Mark's "deserting" them at Pamphylia that he refused to continue on with Barnabus and John Mark (Acts 15:37-40). In Athens, Paul grew exasperated by all of the idols, "so he argued in the synagogue with the Jews and the devout persons, and in the market place every day *with whoever chanced to be there*" (Acts 17:17, emphasis added).

■ ■ ■

### Natural Virtues of the Choleric

- Strong will
- Confidence
- Courage
- Independence

- *Purposefulness*
- *Magnanimity*

■ ■ ■

## A Little Restraint

In addition to their love for debate and their fiery spirit, cholerics tend to be strong-willed, confident, independent, persistent, and courageous.[7] They are expansive and magnanimous, energetically juggling many projects and quick to learn and apply new skills. They are practical and inclined to doing rather than thinking. In fact, this last point often gets them in trouble, as they speak first and think later, or plunge into some activity wholeheartedly only to discover that it was a mistake. Of course, they won't admit this.

Cholerics can be so intent on achieving their goals that they mow down others in the process; they can be domineering and outspoken, prideful and impatient. They hate to admit they are wrong, and they hate to leave for tomorrow what they can accomplish today, even when they ought to show a little restraint.[8]

Cholerics need to grow in the virtues of humility, obedience, patience, and compassion. Because they are mentally agile and by nature motivated, they sometimes lack sympathy for those who are more sensitive, hesitant, or timid. Their pride leads them to overestimate their own talents and to be impatient with others, or to look with disdain on them. Their quick temper and outspoken tongue needs taming, and though it will be a real cross for them, they will need to apologize sincerely when they are in the wrong. Begin this training when they are small: look for opportunities to demonstrate how to graciously apologize and ask forgiveness. Because they tend to think they are right and everyone else is in the wrong, it can be an uphill battle.

One strategy might be to propose a family-wide pursuit of a virtue each month: if the whole family is working on the virtue of humility, for example, the choleric might not take it as such a devastating blow to his pride. And when modeling this and any other virtue, remember to use calm reasoning when the choleric is in the wrong: it will work better than simply yelling, "You apologize *now!*" The latter tends to result in further digging in or else the inevitable "*Sorry!*" — which sounds anything but.

## *Developing Patience*

Every young child needs to learn patience, but the choleric struggles especially with this virtue. Small children tend to be impatient and may interrupt their parents because they simply can't wait to tell them something important; this is acceptable at the age of five or six, but not at age ten.[9] David Isaacs, author of *Character Building*, suggests that parents help their impatient children learn to calm themselves by helping them develop interior peace. Teach them to contemplate nature by listening to the wind rustle the leaves, smelling a sweetly scented honeysuckle, or sitting quietly while observing the night sky. Give them age-appropriate tips on ways to spend time in quiet contemplation without the interruption of cell phones and TV. Help them enter God's presence through the sacraments and prayer.

Cholerics respect strong, authoritative leaders who are clearly in charge, such as teachers, coaches, and scout leaders.

But they often make decisions without getting prior approval and will question the decisions of those in charge — especially if they view those decisions as wrong.

Cholerics' tendency to argue is likely to be viewed as insubordination or willful disobedience. Parents can help their assertive children learn how to address conflicts and bring up alternate suggestions in a *respectful* way. When they interrupt and yell, "You're *wrong!*" or "I didn't do it!" or "That's ridiculous!" give them examples of polite, respectful disagreement. You might even try role-playing when everyone is in a good mood. Then when the time comes — and tempers are flaring — a more polite (and well-rehearsed) script will prevent the argument from escalating.

Teach cholerics the value of servant leadership. Rather than leading by command and control, offer them opportunities to serve. Put them in charge of the younger siblings when shopping or sightseeing; give them opportunities to volunteer with service organizations or to be a teacher's aide for religious education at the parish; get them involved in a "clean up" campaign in the neighborhood; have them walk or run for a charity.

Typically, cholerics don't enjoy babysitting and can become impatient, bossy, and demanding with their younger charges. Nonetheless, babysitting, tutoring, coaching, and mentoring younger children are important occasions for the young choleric to learn empathy and compassion. When they are very small, begin to teach these virtues by asking, "How would you feel if someone did that to you?" or by observing, "That lady must have been having a really bad day herself, and that is why she is so grouchy."

Without a supernatural focus and a sense of dependence on God's grace, cholerics can become mini-dictators. Parents can help direct their choleric child's abundant energy and strength of will toward serving others and seeking God's will. Eventually, though it may take many years, they will begin to understand and appreciate the beatitudes, especially: "Blessed are the meek, for they shall inherit the earth" (Matthew 5:5). With your help, your choleric child will gradually learn that he is not always right, is not the final arbiter of all disputes, and is not the center.

## Saint in the Making

So don't worry, your demanding choleric has what it takes to become a saint. As the revered spiritual writer Henri Joly wrote in *The Psychology of the Saints*, "Easy temperance and absence of desires and passions are not necessarily among the natural virtues that sanctity builds upon."[10] Many saints had strong, fiery, or extremely difficult temperaments. St. Ignatius Loyola was a choleric who practiced heroic virtue in overcoming the weaknesses of his temperament. St. Jerome was noted for his opinionated, argumentative, and disagreeable temperament. St. Teresa of Ávila, the great mystic and doctor of the Church, had been quite the impetuous young choleric in her younger years.

As a child, Teresa was impulsive and headstrong. After reading about the Crusades, she promptly packed her bags and ran away from home — dragging her brother Rodrigo with her — in the hope that together they would die a martyr's death. Later, as a reformer and founder of the Discalced Carmelites, she was energetic, witty, driven, and down to earth.

As Joly explains, St. Teresa's "dislike of the 'way of fear,' especially of 'servile fear,' in the service of God, came, in great measure, from the natural character which she had inherited."[11] Her down-to-earth temperament proved that her prayer life was a divine gift, and her active, fighting spirit was put to the service of God and the Church.

## Cholerics: Made for the Challenge

A choleric saint is one who, for the sake of the Lord, willingly undergoes humiliations and provocations without retaliating, who seeks God's will, who practices mercy and forgiveness, and who humbly serves the poor and despised. As Father Hock wisely recommends: "In the training of the choleric child one must place high ideals before him; appeal to his good will, his sense of honor, his abhorrence of the vulgar, his temporal and eternal welfare; influence him voluntarily to correct his faults and develop his good qualities."[12]

Cholerics can step up to a challenge, even in the spiritual life. In our house, Christmas Day is especially sacrosanct, and nothing supersedes this special family occasion. When their cousins left on Christmas Day for a surprise trip to Hawaii, our children shook their heads in wonder and said they would rather stay home. But one Christmas, Art offered Sam and Lucy the opportunity to serve dinner to the homeless, taking a big chunk out of their Christmas Day. Both jumped at the chance, and Lucy was particularly proud of the opportunity to serve the poor in this challenging way.

■ ■ ■

### Virtues for the Choleric to Work On

- Patience
- Compassion

- *Humility*
- *Obedience*
- *Empathy*

■ ■ ■

## MELANCHOLICS AND VIRTUE

A melancholic child seems most naturally suited to the interior life: he is reflective, serious, sensitive, and by nature, pious.[13] Even as a small child, the melancholic will show a strong preference for the ideal. He is drawn to what is right, true, and just. He has a keen sense of fairness and what *ought* to be. Often this can cause frustration — not only for himself but also for his family and friends. The earnest melancholic is likely to be the child forcing everyone to play the game according to the rules, tattling to Mom, or crying because the game was not fair. Or he may simply spend most of his time playing by himself or reading. He values quality, not quantity, of friends. He is devoted to his few, best friends.

■ ■ ■

### Natural Virtues of the Melancholic

- *Order*
- *Discipline*
- *Reflection*
- *Perseverance*
- *Obedience*
- *Piety*
- *Sensitivity*

■ ■ ■

The melancholic is naturally inclined to the virtues of order, discipline, obedience, and contemplation. He is serious in outlook and sometimes finds other children's hilarity and high jinks perplexing. He will follow the rules and insist that others follow them, sometimes to the point of inflexibility or even scrupulosity. He may be hesitant and unsure when starting something new. He wants to do everything just right — perfectly — and fears not being able to do so, or he becomes overwhelmed in the process of trying.

Melancholics are critical of others and of themselves. In short, they tend to see the glass as half-empty, rather than half-full. According to Father Christian Kappes: "The melancholic needs to experience tenderness and love of her soul created and cherished by God."[14]

## Instilling Confidence, Growing in Prayer

Parents have the task of gently encouraging the virtues of confidence (trust in God), joy, and charity. Confidence will help the melancholic fight against the tendency to timidity and fear, especially in the face of something new. Melancholics would rather everything remain the same, even if that is not the best option, than undertake a scary new project or attend a new school or apply for a new job, especially if they fear they might fail. Striking off in a new direction, initiating a new approach, or thinking outside the box may strike fear in a melancholic's orderly and cautious soul.

The confidence we want to instill is the confidence that is grounded in hope, trusting always in God's providence. God knows what we need, even if we don't; he will provide for us and guide us in the right path. But melancholics don't always grasp this. They take the less optimistic path and often think that everything ultimately depends on them: if they don't get it just right, then it's going to fail. This is why a strong prayer life is essential to the melancholic. In prayer, he begins to know the depth and breadth of God's love for him. Father Hock wrote that "in communication with God the melancholic finds a deep and indescribable peace."[15]

Your melancholic child will take readily to prayer and the sacraments — his naturally serious nature already inclines to reflection, quiet, and solitude. Of course, when they are small children, busily playing with their siblings and friends, this may not be immediately apparent. But you will notice that the melancholic child can spend hours in quiet imaginary games without demanding a playmate or to be entertained. He also loves to be read to, to draw, to listen to music, and he is contented and soothed by evening prayers. If you cultivate these natural tendencies, the seeds for a fertile interior life will find root, as your melancholic grows older.

The many beautiful Catholic traditions for the family are also a great comfort and source of joy for the melancholic child, who loves to participate with his parents. Include your sensitive melancholic in artistic spiritual activities, such as making rosaries or ornaments for the Jesse Tree, lighting the Advent candles, baking Lenten pretzels, or creating cards for newly baptized babies in the parish. Help him understand the strength and supernatural confidence that can be found in the sacraments, without which he might otherwise cling to a friend or seek refuge in solitary activities.

## Cultivating Joy

Because melancholics are serious and careful, they have a greater sense of responsibility — especially if they are both melancholic *and* the firstborn — than children of other temperaments. David Isaacs, author of *Character Building*, cautions parents *not* to take advantage of this natural tendency by piling on more and greater responsibilities, but to be aware of the areas in which these children might be lacking: cheerfulness, flexibility, or sociability, for example.[16] To add heavier responsibilities might contribute to anxiety in this child.

You can counter the tendency to fretfulness in the melancholic and enable him to experience a greater level of joy by helping him cultivate a spirit of gratitude. Sometimes the negative or mistrustful attitude of the melancholic leads to a lack of thankfulness and eventually a sense of discouragement and despondency. The sensitive melancholic can fall easily into berating himself for his failures, and he can begin to flounder in a sea of self-doubt and self-recrimination. He becomes so caught up inside his own head that he loses perspective, taking a bleak view of everything, including his own life. Melancholics need to consciously fight against a negative self-image and negative thoughts that can steal his joy. Becoming aware of his thought patterns — for example, consciously noting when he starts making negative generalizations or begins worrying about potential future mishaps — will help him be more realistic, present-oriented, and joyful.

Deliberately counting your blessings is a good antidote to this negativity and unhappiness. Have your child take time each day to write down three things that went well. Consider adopting the dinnertime tradition of one family we know: they go around the table, and each person mentions one thing he or she is grateful for that day. Another family started the tradition of keeping "gratitude journals," in which they write each night before bed. What does *not* usually help is barking at the fretful, worried melancholic, "Why can't you just snap out of it?" Your child is likely to feel even more worried and begin to obsess about the problem.

Another avenue to joy is in serving those who are less fortunate. Wrapped in his own world, a melancholic can forget that others are suffering far more than he. Serving others cheerfully can help bring him outside himself and increase his happiness. Researchers have found that we can grow in happiness by being thankful and by performing acts of kindness.

When we consciously choose to be grateful, even in difficult circumstances, our ability to see the good in life is strengthened. With time and practice, seeing your cup half-*full*, can become a mental habit, even for the naturally pessimistic melancholic.

## Growing in the Virtue of Charity

Finally, melancholics need encouragement to grow in the virtue of charity. Their sensitivity is a true gift, but it needs to be focused outward to help others in a spirit of compassion and empathy. Too often, the introverted melancholic directs his sensitivity inward. He feels hurt by a harsh word, an uncertain glance, or a perceived slight. He worries, broods, or complains. Melancholics don't realize how their grumpy attitude or critical words hurt others. When they correct a friend's mistakes, they might speak angrily, harshly, or sarcastically — without intending to be hurtful. They often take a condescending tone while demanding service or obedience, which doesn't endear them to subordinates or siblings, and they fail to express gratitude when someone helps them with a task. In short, they don't realize how their negativity infects the atmosphere.

By doing small charitable acts at home and in their neighborhood, melancholics will gradually discover that service to others lifts their spirits. They will also learn that the way we treat one another — our gentleness, kindness, and tone of voice — is vital. St. Teresa of Ávila says that a melancholic can be bitter and unforgiving toward others because he is focused too much on other people's faults and because he secretly wants his own way.[17] The melancholic is too shy to inflict his will on others in the same way a choleric would. However, he can make it known in more subtle ways: eye rolling, heavy sighs, critical comments, silent treatment, refusal to budge, sarcasm, and condescension.

Despite their sometimes grumbling, aloof ways, the melancholic is a faithful, true, and devoted friend. She is steadfast and loyal, self-sacrificing, and always empathetic. Father Hock says that the melancholic is a true benefactor, trustworthy, and a good counselor in difficulties.[18] Father Christian Kappes, in his article "The Melancholic Temperament and the Catholic Soul," makes an intriguing point that we believe is quite accurate. The melancholic, in her search for true friendship, should take care not to become an "attachment" to another person's ego. This is a wise warning for those melancholics who are so loyal and devoted that they do not realize they have been co-opted by someone of a strong temperament who seeks only a companion to feed his ego.[19]

The melancholic — more comfortable in solitary or clearly defined activities — might need encouragement to take on service-oriented projects. When the melancholic is very young, help her extend herself. Bake a batch of cookies together and bring them to a new neighbor; make a card and take it to someone who is sick; decorate a cake for a younger sibling;

arrange flowers and set the table for dinner. Dad can walk his young melancholic son to baseball practice, introduce him to his coach or to his scout leader, smooth the way for altar serving by introducing him to the pastor, or invite another dad and son over for an evening of cooking s'mores in the backyard fire pit.

Serving the poor, volunteering at the parish, taking on a leadership role with a Catholic youth club, or helping a local pro-life politician are all ways a melancholic can get outside himself. Though he may balk at doing something that involves a group or leadership — and may prefer doing something solitary, such as stuffing envelopes — it is wise to encourage the more social activities: collecting baby items for a ministry to needy moms or joining the parish youth group, for example. The first step is always the hardest. But once he takes it, your melancholic will be faithful and committed, capable of self-denial and long suffering.

## A Sensitive, Heroic Saint

At times, you may worry about your young melancholic: when he is little and being teased or ignored by neighborhood cliques, when he is having a high school meltdown about his homework, or when he is painfully struggling to make an important life decision. But your serious and often brilliant melancholic will persevere through these trials of life.

Edith Stein, the gifted philosopher and theologian who became St. Teresa Benedicta of the Cross, was perhaps a melancholic. She struggled with hypersensitivity and anxiety, and as a young girl she was temperamental, high strung, and strong willed. She found it "humiliating" to be a child and found her niche only in school: "In school people took me seriously."[20] She also had a gift for friendship and carefully nurtured her relationships with others.

Once she converted to Catholicism (she was a non-practicing Jew), she immediately wanted to enter the Carmelites because she was so drawn to the contemplative life. Her spiritual directors, however, advised her to continue teaching and speaking. She wrote, "I ... thought that leading a religious life meant giving up all earthly things and having one's mind fixed on divine things only."[21] Eventually, she heroically offered her own life for the sake of her Jewish (and Christian) countrymen, dying at Auschwitz concentration camp.

■ ■ ■

### Virtues for the Melancholic to Work On

- *Supernatural confidence*
- *Charity*
- *Courage*
- *Joy*
- *Gratitude*
- *Flexibility*

■ ■ ■

## SANGUINES AND VIRTUE

Your chipper, enthusiastic, and busy sanguine possesses some of the most endearing natural virtues: optimism, friendliness, generosity, and forgiveness. He easily makes friends with young and old alike, communicates readily and often, and is funny, affectionate, and helpful. Sanguines are so friendly and trusting that when they are very young, they need to be cautioned about taking rides with strangers. Except nobody is really a "stranger" to a sanguine, so he needs to be under strict rules not to get into a car or go off with anyone who isn't his mom, dad, sister, brother, or other well-known friend or relative. On one occasion, we were at a coffee shop during the NCAA March Madness, and our sanguine nine-year-old was filling out his brackets for the college basketball tournament. Within ten minutes, several other adults had joined us at our table, discussing their choices with Sam. The sanguine is naturally expressive, outgoing, and charismatic.

As children, sanguines are always busy, and they keep you running; usually any infractions are inadvertent. They don't *mean* to get into trouble; it just seems to happen! They are so lively and impulsive — and impressionable — that they can be imprudent, or go off with a troublemaker, or show off with a practical joke. As Father Hock puts it, "Nobody is so easily seduced, but on the other hand, nobody is so easily converted as the sanguine."[22]

With their active imagination, easily captured attention, and love for pleasure, sanguines can find themselves impulsively following a less-than-virtuous activity without really thinking about it. As Jordan Aumann puts it, "Being readily moved by the impression of the moment, they easily succumb to temptation."[23] They are usually quite contrite, but they may fall into the same situation if they do not thoughtfully reflect on what they are doing. You can carefully (and lovingly) help your child to understand the consequences of his decisions and actions. Guide your sanguine to look beneath the surface to see that all that glitters is not gold.

Relationships are key for the sanguine; he loves his family and friends, and he is naturally considerate, affectionate, forgiving, and fun — all excellent qualities in a good friend. But remember his tendency to superficiality and impulsivity. This means that the sanguine can sometimes make the wrong choice of friends, swayed by a flashy outfit, a fun demeanor, or a fancy house. He doesn't always remember to look a little deeper or to value those qualities that are less immediately gratifying. Further, the sanguine is tempted to place *too much* trust in other people and in immediate pleasures, to the point of going along with the crowd when he knows he shouldn't or denying what he knows to be right in order to please someone else.

David Isaacs says that the virtue of prudence can be encouraged by helping your child learn how to size up a situation, how to judge, and how to make prudential decisions.[24] Do this while he is young — you will not always be there to guide him. A sanguine may be easily tempted, but if he has been practicing how to make wise and virtuous choices, then he should soon correct himself. This is critical when he is a teen who is spending more time away from home and in the company of school friends or work cohorts.

Parents can ask their sanguine: "When your friend didn't show up as he said he would, how did you feel? Being trustworthy is important in a true friend, don't you think?" or "Persevering through those grueling two-a-day football practices makes the Friday-night victory even sweeter, doesn't it?"

■ ■ ■

### *Natural Virtues of the Sanguine*

- *Joy*
- *Generosity*

- *Enthusiasm*
- *Sociability*
- *Optimism*
- *Flexibility*

■ ■ ■

## *Learning Self-Control*

Parents can help their sanguine child discover that there are many times when delaying immediate gratification results in true happiness, lasting joy, and real peace. Children don't realize that when their parents go to work, clean the house, cook dinner, take care of their kids, and drive them to school and sports activities, they are not merely doing what they *like* but what they ought, and that these very activities give them a greater joy.

Share your feelings about your own challenges in finding a healthy balance of work and play. Learning to regulate our desires is part of learning self-control. In this wealthy, consumer-oriented society, this is very difficult. Consider initiating discussions around the dinner table: "What does it mean to be materialistic? How should we treat all people? Do we really need so many things when so many people are suffering?" Perhaps the family could sacrifice some treat — or the child could put aside his allowance — to help someone in need.

Sanguines struggle with perseverance in spiritual matters, as well as with daily chores and academics. Give your sanguine age-appropriate tasks or projects, keeping tabs along the way and insisting on completion. For example, chores such as these:

- Cleaning his room thoroughly.
- Taking out the trash.
- Setting the table.

Or good works:

- Helping a neighbor with yard maintenance.
- Helping make a meal for a friend who is ill and delivering it.
- Writing a letter to Grandma.

Or spiritual practices:

- Praying the Rosary.
- Keeping a prayer journal.
- Reading Scripture every night.

Be sure to point out how much *happier* your sanguine child is when he prays and works hard, completes a project, helps others, and perseveres through difficult times.

Your lively and imaginative sanguine may be especially drawn to the aspects of the faith that appeal to the senses — the sights and smells of a beautiful church with lighted candles, incense, stained-glass windows, statues of the saints, as well as stories with dramatic illustrations and the beautiful rituals of the sacraments. Even if he wants to be an altar server to be with his best friend, rather than from the pure intention of serving the Lord, his love for Christ and the Mass will mature over time. Parents don't need to discourage their sanguine's love for their friends and enthusiasm for fun activities; rather, they can use these as motivating means to take the next step in virtue.

## The Experiential Temperament

Parents of sanguines will tell you (with a heavy sigh) that these children need to learn by experience. They are simply less likely to take your parental word of advice, they do not react well to stern and forbidding restrictions, and they often need to learn by struggling through their own mistakes. This is all the more reason for parents to be clear and firm about their expectations. Parents can help their experiential sanguine learn how to identify what is truly good (instead of mere pleasure), to make prudent choices, and to persevere in doing what is right. It will help if you can relate personal experiences of your own: that time your dad wisely didn't let you hang out with some sketchy kids, the summer you helped out some neighbors, or how you wished you had studied harder in high school. While these anecdotes won't necessarily keep your sanguine from making his own mistakes, they can help plant seeds of wisdom. Your child truly enjoys doing things with you: include him when you volunteer at the homeless shelter, usher at Mass, or visit a sick neighbor. These are all virtue-building and relationship-strengthening experiences.

## Sanguine Saints

St. Peter was probably a sanguine — lovable, but rather impulsive. "I will never betray you, Lord!" he promises. "No, I am not one of them!" he swears when questioned, and then he betrays Jesus three times. At the Transfiguration, he enthusiastically offers: "Let us make three booths" — even though, as Scripture also notes, he said this "not knowing what he said" (Luke 9:33). He impetuously jumps out of the boat to walk on the water but then looks down at the water and, afraid, begins to sink. He falls asleep in the Garden of Olives and then impulsively cuts off the Roman's ear. And of course, there is that great stumbling block to the happy-go-lucky sanguine: the cross. When Jesus announces that he must go to Jerusalem to suffer and die, Peter tells him that he will never let him suffer and die. Jesus replies, "Get behind me, Satan!" (Mark 8:33).

St. Philip Neri is another sanguine saint. He was a lively, joyful child, "a handsome boy with attractive manners and a gay spirit, but sensitive — the kind that quickly wins affection from others," according to one biographer.[25] He had a great sense of humor, was not overly pious as a child, and was perhaps a bit impulsive: noted at his canonization was the time he pushed his sister because she interrupted him and the time he tore up a copy of the family tree.

His cheerfulness and gift for humor may have been natural virtues, but he used these endearing qualities and his penchant for practical jokes to draw souls to Christ. Furthermore, far from being a hindrance to personal holiness, his good humor helped him retain humility and simplicity. He maintained that cheerfulness was a necessary step to making progress in virtue — and as Father Matthews notes in his biography, if St. Philip saw anyone being sad, he would box him on the ears, saying it was the devil he was beating.

Just standing near him would restore a visitor's cheerfulness. Once he cured a fellow priest who was suffering from depression by saying, "Come, let us run together!"[26]

Like St. Philip, St. Peter, and other sanguine saints, your sanguine can grow into a mature adult who serves both God and humanity through the gift of a lively, enthusiastic, joyful, and contagious faith. Enjoy this spirited child, who brings to your family magic and innocence, enthusiasm and spontaneity.

■ ■ ■

### *Virtues for the Sanguine to Work On*

- *Perseverance*
- *Patience*
- *Reflection*
- *Constancy*
- *Self-control*
- *Prudence*

■ ■ ■

## PHLEGMATICS AND VIRTUE

Your sweet phlegmatic child possesses the natural virtues of peacefulness, patience, docility, serenity, and gentleness. He plays unselfishly with his siblings and friends, follows his parents' directives obediently, and sits quietly in the classroom. With his calm, undemanding disposition, he can be so low-maintenance that you are tempted to leave him to his own devices. But relying too heavily on his natural virtues might lead a parent to neglect building up areas of weakness and can also leave the child with a sense of being taken for granted.

Of all the temperaments, phlegmatics often suffer the most from low self-esteem. They rarely speak up or call attention to themselves, and because of their distaste for interpersonal conflict, they can be too willing to concede another's position. If they are subsequently ignored or overlooked, they may wonder whether they are worthy of notice.

Parents are usually quite relieved to have at least one child with such a calm and agreeable disposition, especially if they have their hands full with a new baby, a needy toddler, a demanding choleric, or a high-energy sanguine. But phlegmatics need some parental coaching, too, even if they don't need reining in, rescuing from impulsive pranks, or soothing after melancholic meltdowns. Phlegmatic children need drawing out, lots of encouragement, and motivating pep talks to discover their true strengths, their vocation, and their leadership skills.

Because they tend to be naturally self-effacing — or simply loathe to push themselves forward — phlegmatics may be reluctant to take an active role in serving others, in speaking the truth, or in standing up for what is right and just. Our phlegmatic was once in a religious club, where he was a quiet yet sincere participant in faith-based activities. He was teased by one of the other, more outgoing and belligerent boys, who made fun of our son's genuine expression of his faith. Our phlegmatic would not speak up against the obnoxious boy, and he preferred to quit the group in disgust. Parents need to be on the lookout for situations like this, where the quiet and gentle nature of the phlegmatic is trampled by more aggressive, outspoken kids.

Parents can model sticking up for oneself, forthright and courageous behavior, and serving the community and the Church. We can use teachable moments from our own lives: "You know, son, I hate to disagree with people at work, but today I took an unpopular stand on an important issue and, while it was hard, I felt a lot better afterward, because I knew I did the right thing!"

Because the phlegmatic is naturally respectful, docile, and patient, he does need this help to learn how to speak up for himself, to be courageous, and to stand up for what is right. We might call this the virtue of holy audacity. Audacity is not rashness but rather a courageous magnanimity that allows a child to take a risk for a higher good. It requires both courage and self-confidence. These are virtues that might be challenging for the naturally self-effacing, retiring phlegmatic. Nonetheless, the phlegmatic may be in the best position to attain the heights of this virtue, with his capacity for unselfish and humble service.

By helping younger siblings, babysitting, or taking on coaching or tutoring jobs, the young phlegmatic will be drawn out of his shell and begin to develop leadership skills. As a teen, our phlegmatic son was in great demand as a coach at a summer day camp because he was one of the very few boys who had patience and good humor with the dozens of rowdy youngsters who would insistently call his name, demand that he play with each of them, and hang on his neck like a human life-preserver in the swimming pool.

■ ■ ■

### Natural Virtues of the Phlegmatic

- Serenity
- Meekness
- Gentleness
- Sincerity
- Patience
- Docility
- Cooperation

■ ■ ■

## *The Angelic (and Phlegmatic) Doctor*

The brilliant St. Thomas Aquinas exhibited many of the traits of the phlegmatic temperament. Neither excitable nor talkative as the sanguines and cholerics, he was careful in speech and thought, and he was detached, dispassionate, and methodical in his arguments. His peers underrated his brilliance — phlegmatics are often underrated by others. They called him "the dumb ox" because of his "obstinate unresponsiveness" — he never showed off his intellectual acumen in debates as the other students loved to do, and he was so slow at responding that they thought he was mentally deficient.

He was also dry witted and trusting, as one story reveals. His friends had played a trick on him, saying, "Look out the window! A flying cow!" St. Thomas fell for it and looked out the window. As everyone laughed, Thomas supposedly replied: "I would rather believe in a flying cow than that my friends would lie to me!"[27] His temperament served him well as a philosopher: he thought things through deeply and thoroughly, never rushing to a conclusion, always carefully giving due consideration to reasonable arguments and objections.

## *Striving for the Best*

Phlegmatics can be tempted to do things simply to please other people, but this quality can be transformed when directed toward God. Their cooperative spirit and their natural sensitivity make them good candidates for altar serving, helping the homebound or infirm, contributing in small, humble ways to serving God and neighbor. When they are encouraged to strive for the best and take on challenging roles, their humility and hard work will allow them to become strong and mature Christian leaders.

■ ■ ■

## Virtues for the Phlegmatic to Work On

- *Confidence*
- *Courage*
- *Audacity*
- *Industriousness*
- *Optimism*

■ ■ ■

\*\*\*

As God revealed to St. Catherine of Siena, he did not give each one of us *every* gift or virtue that we might need in our lives. He says to St. Catherine in the *Dialogue*:

> To one person I give charity as the primary virtue, to another justice, to another humility, to another a live-ly faith or prudence or temperance or patience, and to still another courage. These and many other virtues I give differently to different souls, and the soul is most at ease with that virtue which has been made primary for her.... Thus I have given you reason — necessity, in fact — to practice mutual charity.[28]

God wants us to grow in the understanding that we *need* other people and that we *need* his grace. And by ministering to others, using the graces and gifts we have received from him, we become God's ministers. In this way, we grow in charity and love for God and neighbor.

Each of our precious offspring is a beloved child of God, a unique and unrepeatable person. As parents, we have the awesome challenge of helping each one become the best, most virtuous person he or she can be, and to one day enjoy an intimate friendship with the Lord. Our children need our ministering aid in drawing out their virtues and gifts, and the family provides the perfect opportunity to practice mutual charity and self-giving. It is within the family that our children will first experience the gift of God's saving love and learn to share that precious gift.

## Natural Virtues and Weaknesses

| NATURAL VIRTUES | NATURAL WEAKNESSES |
| --- | --- |
| **Choleric** | |
| Strong will | Prideful |
| Purposeful | Stubborn |
| Resourceful | Domineering |
| Quick learner | Impatient |
| Zeal | Unempathic |
| Self-confident | Quick temper |
| Self-motivated | Outspoken |
| Magnanimous | Always thinks he's right |
| Goal-oriented | Hates to apologize |
| Pragmatic | |
| **Melancholic** | |
| Idealistic | Scrupulous |
| Disciplined | Haughty |
| Orderly | Overly cautious |
| Earnest | Tends to despondency |
| Self-control | Critical, judgmental |
| Careful | Unforgiving |
| Serious, pious | Isolated |
| Deliberate | Suspicious |
| Attention to detail | Worrier |
| Persevering | |
| | (continued on next page) |

## Natural Virtues and Weaknesses
(continued)

| NATURAL VIRTUES | NATURAL WEAKNESSES |
| --- | --- |
| **Sanguine** | |
| Joyful | Intemperate |
| Understanding | Impulsive |
| Friendly | Vain |
| Empathic | Distracted |
| Compassionate | Superficial |
| Helpful | Prone to flattery |
| Generous | Surrenders easily |
| Enthusiastic | Flighty |
| Forgiving | |
| Flexible | |
| **Phlegmatic** | |
| Peaceful | Inclined to passivity |
| Meek | Conflict avoidant |
| Humble | Doesn't speak up |
| Patient | Fear of unknown |
| Merciful | Lacks confidence |
| Sincere | Tends to discouragement |
| Careful | Overly deliberative |
| Methodical | |
| Cooperative | |
| Obedient | |

# Epilogue

*Seeing with the eyes of Christ, I can give to others*
*much more than their outward necessities; I can give*
*them the look of love which they crave.*
Pope Benedict XVI

Parenting is a truly awesome responsibility and a great gift. Each child is unique and unrepeatable, a precious gift from God. Our kids' very distinct temperaments are part of who they are, right from birth, and their temperaments are also a gift from God. Respecting that gift of temperament and beginning to understand how best to motivate, discipline, and love each one is part of our task as parents. Understanding temperament helps us become more loving, forgiving, and helpful to our children.

We parents also have our own unique gifts to share with our children. Knowing ourselves (and our own temperament) is necessary to grow spiritually, as the saints tell us, and to become better parents. As we become more aware of our own temperamental biases, we begin to realize how we can best lead our families to know, love, and serve God, and to one day be happy with him in heaven. By drawing on our own strengths, acknowledging our own temperamental weaknesses, and watching out for areas where these may clash with our kids, we can minimize the battles and daily power struggles.

We discussed that parents have two roles: to establish a relationship with their children and to lead their children so that they might become the persons Christ wants them to be. Most of us (by temperament) lean one way or the other: toward relating or toward leading. But our children need us to be both: good at relating to them and good at leading them. This is not easy, but it is necessary for their growth, and for our own growth as parents. This is taking up our own cross daily, and it is part of how our children help us become holy.

Pope Benedict XVI wrote in his encyclical *Spe Salvi*:

Life is like a voyage on the sea of history, often dark and stormy, a voyage in which we watch for the stars that indicate the route. The true stars of our life are the people who have lived good lives.[1]

We parents want to be those true stars, modeling virtue and love, leading our families to Christ.

Ultimately, our home can become, as Blessed John Paul II said, a "community of life and love," the domestic Church, the place where each person (no matter how small) is respected and valued, where his or her gifts flourish, and where love is discovered and shared.

# Appendix A:
# Temperament and
# Psychological Disorders,
# Physical Disabilities, and
# Other Special Needs

In this book, we do not directly address the wide variety of psychological disorders or physical disabilities that can impact children. Generally, we discuss temperament from the perspective of children who are not suffering from severe disorders or serious physical disabilities. If your child suffers from either, then any treatment or strategy should be made in concert with your child's physician or a professional child psychologist or both. Nonetheless, an understanding of the child's temperament can be very beneficial.

One of the major contributions by psychiatrists Stella Chess and Alexander Thomas was their identification of certain behavior as a "normal extreme of temperament" rather than a disorder or pathology. Temperamental characteristics are not, in themselves, abnormal, nor does temperament *alone* give rise to a disorder. For example, a parent may worry that his sanguine child's distractibility indicates that the child has attention deficit hyperactivity disorder (ADHD). Or there may be a concern that the choleric child's argumentativeness might be oppositional defiant disorder (ODD), or that the melancholic's perseveration and attention to detail is obsessive-compulsive disorder (OCD) or another anxiety disorder.

Chess and Thomas pointed out that there are "normal extremes of temperament" that do not necessarily require professional intervention, though parents should be sensitive to the most effective way of encouraging their child's growth and maturation. Certain mishandling of temperamental reactions (for example, a parent punishing a child for being highly active, overly sensitive, or naturally distractible) might subsequently give rise to a behavioral problem; nonetheless, temperamental characteristics are themselves not abnormal. If you are in doubt as to whether certain behaviors are evidence of a psychological disorder or another emotional problem, you should consult a mental health professional.

When there is a psychological disorder, the child's temperament can be an important consideration in treatment plans. Temperament can inhibit or enhance the effectiveness of some treatments. For example, a melancholic individual suffering from depression or anxiety disorder may take longer in treatment, yet qualities like introspection can be very beneficial. With certain physical disabilities or other special needs, temperament may play a significant role.[1] A disabled child who is highly persistent may ultimately succeed in accomplishing tasks that a less persistent or more easily discouraged child may have given up on or not even undertaken. Other qualities — such as sociability and an easygoing, optimistic outlook — may prove beneficial when students with special needs join their nondisabled peers at school and in extracurricular activities.

# Appendix B:
# Temperament Test for Kids

P arents, take this test (on page 174) with your child (explaining words he doesn't understand), or take it for him. Circle the ONE word in each line that BEST fits. There should be only ONE WORD circled in EACH LINE. Choose the natural, instinctive, consistent tendency — not something he learned in school or at home, or a skill he was taught. You may also take the test yourself, applying the same rules. (Copyright © Art and Laraine Bennett.)

Now, transfer the SAME WORD you circled in EACH LINE of the test to this score sheet (on page 175). You will notice the words are in a different order than they were in the test. After copying all of the circled words from the test to the score sheet (there should be only ONE circled word in each line), you can identify your child's primary (and secondary) temperament based on the temperament (or temperaments) that has the most circled words. There should be a total of twenty-five words, with only ONE WORD in each line.

## TEMPERAMENT TEST

| 1. Talkative | Opinionated | Serious | Easygoing |
|---|---|---|---|
| 2. Self-reliant | Artistic | Charming | Homebody |
| 3. Dependable | Skeptical | Social butterfly | Action-oriented |
| 4. Diplomatic | Charismatic | Commanding | Analytical |
| 5. Argumentative | Hesitant | Lively | Agreeable |
| 6. Sensitive | Indecisive | Decisive | Gregarious |
| 7. Anxious | Short-tempered | Unmotivated | Flighty |
| 8. Assertive | High standards | Sweet | "Class clown" |
| 9. Independent | Trusting | Cautious | Enthusiastic |
| 10. Distractible | Driven | Procrastinating | Worrier |
| 11. Productive | Introspective | Playful | Calm |
| 12. Bossy | Choosy | Quiet | Impulsive |
| 13. Changeable | Easy to please | Hard to please | Stubborn |
| 14. Humble | Realistic | Idealistic | Adventuresome |
| 15. Energetic | Bubbly | Soft-spoken | Organized |
| 16. Spontaneous | Willful | Peacekeeper | Perfectionist |
| 17. Pessimistic | Optimistic | Inoffensive | Determined |
| 18. Goal-oriented | Studious | Forgetful | Obedient |
| 19. Forgiving | Unforgiving | Confrontative | Non-confrontative |
| 20. Impatient | Patient | Interruptive | Moody |
| 21. Prideful | Fickle | Passive | Vengeful |
| 22. Flexible | Dutiful | Detail-oriented | Strategic |
| 23. Team player | Leader | Rule-abiding | Motivator |
| 24. Confident | Daydreamy | Friendly | Cooperative |
| 25. Shy | Placid | Outspoken | Bouncy |

## SCORE SHEET

| Choleric | Melancholic | Sanguine | Phlegmatic |
|---|---|---|---|
| 1. Opinionated | Serious | Talkative | Easygoing |
| 2. Self-reliant | Artistic | Charming | Homebody |
| 3. Action-oriented | Skeptical | Social butterfly | Dependable |
| 4. Commanding | Analytical | Charismatic | Diplomatic |
| 5. Argumentative | Hesitant | Lively | Agreeable |
| 6. Decisive | Sensitive | Gregarious | Indecisive |
| 7. Short-tempered | Anxious | Flighty | Unmotivated |
| 8. Assertive | High standards | "Class clown" | Sweet |
| 9. Independent | Cautious | Enthusiastic | Trusting |
| 10. Driven | Worrier | Distractible | Procrastinating |
| 11. Productive | Introspective | Playful | Calm |
| 12. Bossy | Choosy | Impulsive | Quiet |
| 13. Stubborn | Hard to please | Changeable | Easy to please |
| 14. Realistic | Idealistic | Adventuresome | Humble |
| 15. Energetic | Organized | Bubbly | Soft-spoken |
| 16. Willful | Perfectionist | Spontaneous | Peacekeeper |
| 17. Determined | Pessimistic | Optimistic | Inoffensive |
| 18. Goal-oriented | Studious | Forgetful | Obedient |
| 19. Confrontative | Unforgiving | Forgiving | Non-confrontative |
| 20. Impatient | Moody | Interruptive | Patient |
| 21. Prideful | Vengeful | Fickle | Passive |
| 22. Strategic | Detail-oriented | Flexible | Dutiful |
| 23. Leader | Rule-abiding | Motivator | Team player |
| 24. Confident | Daydreamy | Friendly | Cooperative |
| 25. Outspoken | Shy | Bouncy | Placid |

# Notes

## Introduction

The opening quotation by Father Conrad Hock is from Conrad Hock, *The Four Temperaments* (original 1934), revised edition by Rev. Nicholas M. Wilwers, S.A.C., M.A., S.T.B. (Milwaukee: The Pallottine Fathers, Inc., 1962), p. 7.

1. Jerome Kagan and Nancy Snidman, *The Long Shadow of Temperament* (Cambridge: The Belknap Press of Harvard University, 2004), pp. 11ff.
2. Jerome Kagan has done significant research on temperament, and he has written several books, including *The Temperamental Thread* and *The Long Shadow of Temperament*, which draw on decades of research into this important concept. Of course, Kagan does not use the terms *choleric, melancholic, sanguine,* and *phlegmatic,* but he discusses more general temperament traits.
3. Stella Chess and Alexander Thomas, *Temperament in Clinical Practice* (New York: The Guilford Press, 1986). Chess and Thomas measured sociability by the infant's withdrawal or approach when presented with certain social situations. A slow-to-warm-up toddler, for example, when presented with a room full of strange adults, might climb into her mother's lap and remain there for the duration.
4. University of Wisconsin-Madison, news release (August 11, 2010), http://www.med.wisc.edu/news-events/news/uw-madison-scientists-inherited-brain-activity-predicts-childhood-risk-for-anxiety/28620.

5. University of Washington, "Kids' anxiety, depression halved when parenting styled to personality," cited in http://healthland.time.com/2011/08/09/kids-depression-plummets-when-parents-adapt-to-their-personalities/.
6. For a more in-depth discussion of temperament combinations, please see our book *The Temperament God Gave You* (Manchester, NH: Sophia Institute Press, 2005).

## Chapter 1: Temperament and Your Child

The opening quotation by Father Conrad Hock is from *The Four Temperaments*, p. 12.

1. Where counseling cases are presented, the names and identifying details have been changed and are often composites of real situations; none is exclusively about a particular client. The situations may sound familiar, simply because they represent universal truths about temperament, parents, and children.
2. The Pontifical Council for the Family, *The Truth and Meaning of Human Sexuality* (1995), n. 65.
3. Sara Nelson, "Do Asian Mothers Know Best? An Interview with Amy Chua," *O, The Oprah Magazine* online (January 14, 2011), http://www.oprah.com/relationships/An-Interview-with-Amy-Chua-Battle-Hymn-of-the-Tiger-Mother.
4. *The Truth and Meaning of Human Sexuality*, n. 54.
5. To be more precise, Chess and Thomas say, in *Temperament in Clinical Practice*, that healthy development occurs when there is a goodness of fit between the child's

capacities and characteristics and the "demands and expectations of the environment."

6. *The Long Shadow of Temperament*, p. 32.
7. Inspired by Laura Vaughn Dumochelle.
8. Cf. David Isaacs, *Character Building* (Dublin, Ireland: Four Courts Press, 1984), p. 164. Parents need to develop the virtue of patience.
9. *The Four Temperaments*, p. 35.
10. In fact, a parent of a melancholic or phlegmatic has to be particularly attentive to their child's need for overt appreciation and affection, because these introverted types may not let you know how much they need your verbal and physical expressions of love. Even the extraverted choleric child will sometimes appear so self-sufficient that a parent might not realize how much physical touch and affectionate expressions he truly needs!
11. Peter Drucker, *Managing Oneself* (Boston: Harvard Business School Publishing Corporation, 2008), p. 2.

## Chapter 2: Your Conquering Choleric Child

1. *The Four Temperaments*, p. 17. A key point here is that while people of all temperaments are fully capable of commanding, organizing, and leading, the choleric is naturally so, and this makes him *happy.*
2. Raymond Arroyo, *Mother Angelica* (New York: Doubleday, 2005). These are just two of the many wonderful stories about this energetic, audacious, saintly woman.
3. This story is used with permission from Simcha Fisher, who blogs for the *National Catholic Register* and can also be found at www.simchafisher.com.

4. *Peanuts* © Peanuts Worldwide LLC. Dist. By Universal Uclick. Reprinted with permission. All rights reserved.

5. Researchers studied infants to determine at what age a baby knew he was a distinct person, separate from his mother. By eighteen months, most babies were able to show that they had a sense of self. Around the same time, babies begin to have temper tantrums, with the severity often depending on the level of language ability the child has: the more a child is able to express his wants and needs, the less he has to depend on temper tantrums. The so-called terrible twos are therefore considered to be part of the process of individuation for some children. Cf. José B. Ashford et al., *Human Behavior in the Social Environment: A Multidimensional Perspective, Fourth Edition* (Belmont, CA: Wadsworth, 2010), p. 262.

6. In fact, parents who never allow their children to say no are teaching them that they are powerless against any outside forces, including evil, in the world. See Dr. Henry Cloud and Dr. John Townsend, *Boundaries: When to Say 'Yes,' When to Say 'No,' To Take Control of Your Life* (Grand Rapids, MI: Zondervan, 1992), p. 50.

7. *The Four Temperaments*, p. 25.

8. Rudolf Allers, M.D., Ph.D. *Forming Character in Adolescents* (Fort Collins, CO: Roman Catholic Books, 1940), p. 78.

9. "By free will one shapes one's own life. Human freedom is a force for growth and maturity in truth and goodness" (CCC 1731).

10. Authoritative parenting (which sets limits within a positive, supportive environment) is considered optimal for all temperaments. Authoritative is not the same as authoritarian, which exhibits high demands without the warmth and supportiveness of the authoritative style.

11. *The Four Temperaments*, p. 25.
12. Ibid., pp. 25-26.
13. Ibid., p. 25.

## Chapter 3: Your Moody Melancholic Moppet

1. University of Wisconsin-Madison, "Inherited Brain Activity Predicts Childhood Risk for Anxiety, Research Finds," *ScienceDaily* (August 11, 2010), http://www.sciencedaily .com. /releases/2010/08/100811135037.htm.
2. Jerome Kagan points out that parenting styles as well as other environmental factors such as trauma, war, or economic depression can affect one's emotional development. See *The Long Shadow of Temperament*, pp. 24-26.
3. University of Montreal, "Spare the Rod, Spoil the Child? Excessive Punishment Can Have Lasting Psychological Impact on Children, Researchers Say," *ScienceDaily* (September 21, 2010), http://www.sciencedaily.com/ releases/2010/09/100921144234.htm.

## Chapter 4: Your Spirited Sanguine Sprout

1. Kaiser Family Foundation, *Generation M2: Media in the Lives of 8- to 18-Year-Olds*, 2010.

## Chapter 5: Your Peaceful Phlegmatic Progeny

1. *The Four Temperaments*, p. 46.

## Chapter 6: What's Your Temperament?

The opening quotation by Blessed John Paul II is from John Paul II, 1981 apostolic exhortation *Familiaris Consortio* (on the role of the Christian family in the modern world), n. 39.

1. *Familiaris Consortio*, n. 17.
2. The temperament information in this book will apply just as well to single parents. Though their task is often intensified and may seem, at times, overwhelmingly stressful, we believe God never allows a person to suffer without providing sufficient grace.
3. We also discuss parenting styles in *The Temperament God Gave You* (previously cited) and *The Temperament God Gave Your Spouse* (Manchester, NH: Sophia Institute Press, 2008).
4. Psychological studies show authoritarian parents (who have an inflexible, demanding style) raised children who did well in school but who were anxious and handled frustration poorly. The preferred style is authoritative, which exerts reasonable demands along with responsiveness. See D. Baumrind (1967), "Child care practices anteceding three patterns of preschool behavior," *Genetic Psychology Monographs*, 75 (1), 43-88.
5. Real names and identifying details have been changed to protect privacy.
6. Ben and Annie's story and their communication troubles are described at length in our second book, *The Temperament God Gave Your Spouse*.

## Chapter 7: Parent-Child Temperamental Interaction

The opening quotation by Stella Chess and Alexander Thomas is from *Temperament in Clinical Practice*, p. 26.

1. *Temperament in Clinical Practice*, p. 21.
2. Ibid., p. 26. Chess and Thomas do not, of course, refer to

temperaments by their classical Greek names; instead, they categorize them as "easy," "difficult," or "slow to warm up," and they describe key features such as distractibility, emotionality, sociability, etc.

## Chapter 8: Growing in Virtue

1. *The Truth and Meaning of Human Sexuality*, n. 65.
2. *The Four Temperaments*, p. 15.
3. Ibid.
4. Michael Cawley III et al., "A virtues approach to personality," in *Personality and Individual Differences* 28 (2000), p. 1008.
5. Many of these virtues natural to the four temperaments are discussed in the four-virtue-factor subscales shown in "A virtues approach to personality."
6. Jordan Aumann, O.P., *Spiritual Theology* (Allen, TX: Christian Classics, 1979), p. 143.
7. "A virtues approach to personality," pp. 997-1013.
8. *Spiritual Theology*, p. 144.
9. David Isaacs offers a developmental approach to the virtues in David Isaacs, *Character Building* (Dublin, Ireland: Four Courts Press, 1984), p. 162.
10. Henri Joly, *The Psychology of the Saints* (Fort Collins, CO: Roman Catholic Books, originally published in 1898), p. 48.
11. Ibid., p. 56.
12. *The Four Temperaments*, p. 26.
13. *Spiritual Theology*, p. 142.
14. Christian Kappes, "The Melancholic Temperament and the Catholic Soul" in *The Latin Mass* (Fall 2005), p. 20.

15. *The Four Temperaments*, p. 39.
16. *Character Building*, pp. 77-78.
17. *The Four Temperaments*, p. 43.
18. Ibid., p. 39.
19. See "The Melancholic Temperament and the Catholic Soul."
20. Waltraud Herbstrith, O.C.D., "Edith Stein," www.angelfire.com/ca5/stjoseph/formdocs/edith-stein.htm.
21. Edith Stein (St. Teresa Benedicta of the Cross), as quoted in www.vatican.va/news_services/liturgy/saints/ns_lit_doc_19981011_edith_stein_en.html.
22. *The Four Temperaments*, p. 32.
23. *Spiritual Theology*, p. 141.
24. *Character Building*, pp. 190ff.
25. V. J. Matthews, *Saint Philip Neri* (Rockford, IL: Tan Books, 1984), p. 2.
26. Ibid., p. 80.
27. G. K. Chesterton, *Saint Thomas Aquinas* (New York: Doubleday, 1956).
28. St. Catherine of Siena, *Catherine of Siena: The Dialogue* (Classics of Western Spirituality series) (Mahwah, NJ: Paulist Press, 1980), pp. 37-38.

## Epilogue

The opening quotation by Pope Benedict XVI is from Benedict XVI, 2005 encyclical *Deus Caritas Est* (on Christian love), n. 18.

1. Pope Benedict XVI, 2007 encyclical *Spe Salvi* (on Christian hope), n. 49.

## Appendix A: Temperament and Psychological Disorders, Physical Disabilities, and Other Special Needs

1. *Temperament in Clinical Practice*, pp. 9-10.

# About the Authors

A<small>RT</small> B<small>ENNETT</small> is currently the president and chief executive officer (CEO) of Catholic Charities in the Diocese of Arlington, Virginia. He was also the founder and director of the Alpha Omega Clinics in Maryland and Virginia (2002-2010) and the creator of Unity Restored (www.UnityRestored.com), a website designed to help those afflicted by pornography. He has more than twenty-five years' experience in the mental health field and is a frequent speaker on marriage and family issues.

L<small>ARAINE</small> B<small>ENNETT</small> has a master's degree in philosophy and writes for Catholic Match and the Catholic News Agency's Catholic Womanhood site.

Together, the Bennetts co-authored two popular books on temperament (*The Temperament God Gave You* and *The Temperament God Gave Your Spouse*) in addition to their book *The Emotions God Gave You*. The Bennetts have lived in California and in Germany, and they currently live in Northern Virginia. Art and Laraine have been married for thirty-four years and have four children — one of each temperament type!